Freedom Reread

REREADINGS

REREADINGS

EDITED BY NICHOLAS DAMES AND JENNY DAVIDSON

Short and accessible books by scholars, writers, and critics, each one revisiting a favorite post-1970 novel from the vantage point of the now. Taking a look at novels both celebrated and neglected, the series aims to display the full range of the possibilities of criticism, with books that experiment with form, voice, and method in an attempt to find different paths among scholarship, theory, and creative writing.

Freedom

REREAD

L. GIBSON

COLUMBIA UNIVERSITY PRESS

New York

Columbia University Press
Publishers Since 1893
New York   Chichester, West Sussex
cup.columbia.edu
Copyright © 2023 Columbia University Press

All rights reserved

Library of Congress Cataloging-in-Publication Data
Names: Gibson, L. (Lane), 1987– author.
Title: Freedom reread / L. Gibson.
Description: New York : Columbia University Press, [2023] | Series:
Rereadings | Includes bibliographical references and index.
Identifiers: LCCN 2022027238 (print) | LCCN 2022027239 (ebook) |
ISBN 9780231188920 (hardcover ; acid-free paper) | ISBN 9780231188937
(trade paperback ; acid-free paper) | ISBN 9780231548076 (ebook)
Subjects: LCSH: Franzen, Jonathan. Freedom. |
LCGFT: Literary criticism.
Classification: LCC PS3556.R352 F74345 2023 (print) | LCC PS3556.R352
(ebook) | DDC 813/.54—dc23/eng/20220718
LC record available at https://lccn.loc.gov/2022027238
LC ebook record available at https://lccn.loc.gov/2022027239

Columbia University Press books are printed on permanent and durable
acid-free paper.
Printed in the United States of America

Cover design: Julia Kushnirsky
Cover illustration: Henry Sene Yee

CONTENTS

Freedom Reread

1

COMING DOWN ON FRANZEN

He liked them, was the trouble, Franzen's books.

The Corrections you could set aside. *There* was a great novel, lower-case *g*, small *n*, not—or not only—a Great Novel in the dense, door-stoppy, rankable sense of *V.* or *Rabbit, Run.* From those ponderous ores, his available mining apparatus extracted scant pleasure; to read them was to lug attention by sledge over Gethen's own terrain.

If you really wanted to hear him yak, you could mention *Strong Motion, The Discomfort Zone.* For the *Harper's* Essay and "Farther Away," he had temporal eons, stadia of space. A salon on *Kraus Project*, a *Purity* panel? He'd clear the dates. If Franzen had spilled spleen in the *New Yorker* on any topic, even—especially—birds, hand it here.

What a terrier feels when it plunges after a flung Frisbee, he felt for, over, at Franzen. He tasted feist, which had the high-fructose, caffeinated tang of a full-calorie R.C. Cola. When the toy gave under his incisors, he gloried; when it sprang back, he'd exalt. "Plenty," went the song, was "never enough."

As his Franzen fixation wagged him doggishly, so did a certain sort of question posed in reference to this author. Its querents, those he encountered in dives and dining rooms, meant generosity, he thought, each time they inquired "where he came down on" Jonathan Franzen, or Christopher Nolan, or Paul-Thomas Anderson, or *frères* Coen.

Flat as an abattoir's counter on which slabs of opinion were laid out for carving came these asks. Afterward, a hush descended, as sudden and pure as the wake of a prodded mute button or a raised dam. It was silence only, unadorned by any nicety; head cocked, bare of affirmatives, impatience dawning behind cumulous puzzlement, like a Turner sky.

He had attended elementary school and read *Dune*, learned in these arenas that even spitted saliva could constitute a tribute, a "gift of your body's moisture," in certain milieux.[1] Recently arrived from another realm, still blinking in the pale gleam of Terra's single sun, he tried to accept in that spirit these questions and the silence then allowed to follow—almost to gape, a lawn-and-leaf bag held open for verbal cascade.

His replies, over whatever territory they rambled or meandered, met with the phrase "deep cut"—not, in this case, a compliment—or some interjection along the lines of, "Wait, so, do you like this guy, or no?"

His gusto for holding forth on the subject of Jonathan Franzen extended forever, toward a vanishing point whose habit of receding mirrored the retreat of his listeners.

Why had they scattered, like driven grouse?

From research conducted in the field—bars—and podcast-based armchair anthropology, he came eventually to conclude that this sort of talk did have an etiquette, which doubled as its rhetorical mode. It was a simple one, distillable to two terse fiats: Hold the floor. Have a take.

The pause formed a runway—a helipad, more like. His chance had come to hold the floor. If he had a take, a pitch, an angle, a ranking, the time was now.

He was, alas, more airship than chopper. Asked his opinion about cultural works, he tended to mass mounds of evidence like bright pigment or rack points back and forth like abacus beads, the better to consider their near-parity. If one strand disrupted a pattern, there halted his loom.

To the cleared throat of rising impatience, he might delay by scrutinizing some minute detail, as through a jeweler's loupe, or squandering his listener's credit on extended it's-likes or what-ifs. This did not resolve ambivalence, and none of it was quick.

To have come down on Jonathan Franzen at the frequency requested would have required him to metamorphose into a personal avalanche, a targeted downpour.

Instead, when queried, he *comme çi*'d, *comme ça*'d. Even his briefest attempt at sum-up—"There's gas in JF's car, but where is he going?"—declined to declare.

Aloud, he dodged; inwardly, thought. Where, indeed, did he "come down on" Franzen? Was Jonathan Franzen "one of his guys," even one of his "all-time top ten," or five, or three? Did he like this guy, or no?

What sort of allegiance did one confer, precisely, in proclaiming a contender in any arena *one's guy*, he wondered—was it to grant a vassal's fealty, a bettor's backing, a friend's affection, a rival's challenge?

He had heard Whoopi Goldberg coach a nun's choir through their theistically modified version of the Motown standard "My Guy," Rufus Wainwright declare himself, in folky earnest, a "One Man Guy." Who those guys were, whose were his, he understood.

Via 007 and le Carré, he'd come to suspect that some of an assassin's or spy's guys were outright enemies, their backs one's target. Brits didn't use this term, per se, but the gist held. As they watched Bobby Flay strut through the Food Network program *Throwdown*, his dad said off-hand that there were bad wrestlers, whom it was pleasurable to root against, as a planned, predictable part of the show. Even those must be someone's guys, he thought—whose, though, he couldn't have said. Had they fans, too, like the heroes?

And what about him—was he "a Franzen guy" or even "a huge Franzen guy," as he'd so often been presumed? Was that different—the lighter, more pallish "guy" an equivalent of "admirer," "devotee"—or didn't it work that way? Did it matter whether Franzen was his guy or he, Franzen's? Did power shift with the possessive, or were they the same, a sort of tautology, the way "Bernie bros" were—well, who could say?

He puzzled over which better described their relationship. Was he authorizing Franzen to act on his behalf, as when the big man on the cell block had backed Luke's boast to eat fifty eggs? Or was he Franzen's agent, the author's surrogate in dinner-party lit discourse?

His relation to Franzen manifested less as allegiance or loyalty than as an obsessional interest in which elements of like and dislike sparked flintily against each other or combined to alchemical effect. "Jonathan Franzen, whom I loathe and adore," ran his personal *odi et amo*. Neither verb could be removed any more than you could sieve rye from a Manhattan or siphon off vermouth.

He disapproved—of Franzen per se, of his own JF penchant—and also clung to his own displeasure, at once proof of and proof against that same affection. His weakness for Franzen stood out in relief against it, lay submerged beneath it, stood firm against it like the immovable object against an irresistible force. How great must that affection be, he marveled, to yank where he balked.

What was Franzen to him? Not "guilty pleasure," surely, when guilt was pleasure's guarantor. Nor "problematic fave"—the problem *was* the fave, its business end.

It would have been so simple to say less about Jonathan Franzen. It was patent, from the easy way some people said, "Oh, him," that not everyone who encountered this author's work then brought him up in therapy, on a dating app, or to the unfortunate passenger assigned a neighboring seat.

Others seemed not refer to Franzen so frequently, so familiarly, that acquaintances assumed he was known personally to the narrator, on some frosty, frenemy-adjacent terms that merited a surname. The question "And how is Jonathan Franzen?" began to greet him, casually as a "Howsitgoin'."

"Is this someone you live with?" an overhearer might inquire. In time, he made a bit of it—Franzen the only person he'd podded with during lockdown, Franzen the incorrigible roommate who occupied too much space in his apartment, left messes, squabbled over the thermostat.

Though he assessed himself altogether likelier than JF to ghost on polite texts about the chore wheel, treat ne'er-unpacked grocery bags as auxiliary, movable cabinet space, drape every seat with laundry, the Franzen he sketched behaved boorishly, in the manner of a sitcom husband, with dashes of dorm-room tetch.

Most of his *stories took the form of complaints, and yet nobody doubted that* he *adored* Jonathan Franzen. More and more, he came to sound like someone *bemoaning* his *gorgeous jerky boyfriend. As if* he *were proud of having* his *heart trampled by him: as if* his *openness to this trampling were the main thing, maybe the only thing,* he *cared to have the world know about* (*Freedom*, 8).

"Isn't that your person?" asked a friend who'd heard this writer interviewed. He'd absorbed this term, *one's person*, in a specific, Shonda Rhimesian sense; could not countenance Franzen's relation to him in terms of Meredith's to Cristina.

"I wouldn't say my *person*, exactly," he'd objected, and trumpeted the exchange to everyone he knew.

Jonathan Franzen—who'd been formerly, famously obsessed with nineteenth-century novels and twentieth-century rotary phones, stanned lately for twenty-first-century birds—now fascinated him. Franzen, whose *territory is big shames and big anxieties* (Brown), had awakened—yep, pretty much.

There were less embarrassing ways to feel about this writer's fiction than the way he felt—any other—and containers that better befitted the frets he stashed in Franzen's books—he couldn't have named a worse. Further, were someone then to call him on his *merde*, the roster of people he'd have preferred to the author of *Freedom* approached eight billion at a vertiginous pace.

When, with zero provocation, you gave vent to gales of ire at Jonathan Franzen, a constant, flatulent stream, hot and foul as a subway's updraft, how much more embarrassing—worse than the Franzen fixation itself, the obsession with what it meant, the preoccupation with others' opinions of it—then to receive help from, take solace in, the novels of Jonathan Franzen.

As he had. Through Franzen's fiction, he reentered a state, repose its posture, in which external appearance and interior awareness sharply diverged: recollection resembled amnesia, companionship looked lonesome, focus mimicked distraction. Set like windows into a world that went wall-still around their pages' casings, these novels held him rapt. He couldn't have told whether he peered into or out of—only that they held his gaze.

Each had its angle of recline, its *isola* of bunk or divan on which he stretched in solitude, unlone. He spent Christmas at the Lamberts' one Thanksgiving, *The Corrections* slung across his torso, heavy as another limb atop the mohair throw. A sedan did seventy, its backseat cradling his body, but all he saw, that trip, was a strip of gray-vinyl sky over *Freedom*'s boards. Too swollen for sherbet, mono-bound abed, he swallowed *Purity*, tome propped *schloss*-like on his knees' ridge.

They recalled, these absorptive sprees, his childhood fantasies of astral projection or the dollhouse's plastic avatars whose proxy stories were expressed in vital miniature. Reading, once he learned, was like that, too: body's systems held at low idle, senses anaesthetized to their surrounds, faculties tethered to flesh by only the slenderest cord.

As a young one, he'd discovered that there were hatches, everywhere, out of wherever you were, that perception's corridor was exit-dense, its walls bored with crawlspaces into which one's thinking and feeling core could burrow. He'd found that fictional worlds could act as lead-lined chambers for the safe deposit of intrapersonal material that, when let to fester—in the chest, in the gut—slit tissue, serrated cells.

He'd conceived of his corpus then as a station where imagination and intellect docked, a supply point on the surface of some system's volatile Io, a site to refuel before venturing toward more habitable spheres. Seen from that angle, a story's realism felt less convincing decoy of, more viable alternative to, reality lived primarily—essence, not sim. If this was immersion, he hadn't lungs at all, but gills.

He'd harbored, and made for himself a harbor within, the notion—or pretense or wish—that he *didn't really have a body at all*, but some contraption *more like an armature of coat-hanger wire with a few key sensory parts attached to it*, considered himself *all idea, like a thing drawn by Joan Miró* (*Purity*, 345).

Two-D, a penned sketch, this self of his? Certainly: he'd have said it resembled something felt-tipped onto a transparency, which—given a suitably sized screen, a socket with juice, a projector set atop its creaking cart—could be illumined to human dimensions, a seeming of someone that, he'd thought, looked substantial enough.

One's being, did it reside in the see-through sheet of acetate, the drawn design, the lamplit figure thrown through dimness? How about the humming motor, the plug's prongs, the steel-shelved base whose stern listed on its tipsy wheel?

The person stressed by these questions, whom the diagrammable portion of the world most suited, it calmed to consult a chart that labeled an overhead projector's components, it pleased to learn to call the luminous surface a "stage glass," it comforted subvocally to form the Fresnel lens's name.

That metaphor's parts wouldn't sit, wouldn't settle—this, too, served him, for a time. What with picture denying the existence of filament and lens, cart claiming to know nothing of cord, outlet disavowing what it fed—was this *How* Someone *Came to Be Nowhere?*

2

"All, BUT UNDERNEATH"

They might have been molded by Playmobil, of beige plastic. Mom, dad, daughter, son. House, yard, car. Dog (or no dog). American Nuclear Family, white hetero-bourgeois edition. They were perfect, this family. Which perfect, though? Were they Too Perfect, or Not as Perfect as They Wanted Us to Think? Did No One Suspect a Thing, or was Something Like This Bound to Happen All Along?

Freedom opens on a scandal, investigation in search of crime. It concerns Patty and Walter Berglund and their children, Jessica and Joey. The Berglunds—No Dog, Too Perfect, Something Like This Was Bound to Happen All Along—have departed Ramsey Hill, the St. Paul neighborhood they helped to gentrify, for DC. Walter has, since their move, snarled himself in a professional snafu, word of which arrives on the doorsteps of Barrier Street, his former address, via a *New York Times* exposé. "His old neighbors," qualms the novel's opening paragraph, "had some difficulty reconciling the quotes about him in the *Times* ('arrogant,' 'high-handed,' 'ethically compromised') with the generous, smiling, red-faced 3M employee they remembered pedaling his commuter bicycle up Summit Avenue in February snow" (*Freedom*, 3). Persuade these two Walters to congrue, however, they will. "Then again," pivots the paragraph's end, "there had always been something not quite right about the Berglunds" (3).

Current journalism ruffles old scuttlebutt: the news of Walter's ordeal prompts retrospective review of his family's tenure on Barrier

Street, completing a first pass at *Freedom*'s plot. As young parents—an ecoconscious corporate lawyer and a self-effacingly funny and capable former basketball star—he and Patty renovate a rundown Victorian in which they raise two children, Jessica the responsible, well-rounded achiever to Joey's casuistical capitalist. Adolescence ushers in cyclonic disruption chez Berglund. Patty weathers intervals of heavy drinking and depression, briefly revives during a lakeside summer away. Parent-child clashes culminate in Joey's decamping next door to live with the family of Connie Monaghan, his girlfriend. Walter changes jobs, leaving 3M for the Nature Conservancy, then entering the employ of a mysterious "megamillionaire" (186), Vin Haven, and moving the family east.

Franzen's prose can abseil into the cranny or crevasse between a character and their self-awareness, sound ease or ill-content beneath a marital pause. At its outset, however, *Freedom* lodges a ways down Barrier Street, at some houses' remove from its central cast. The opening section—entitled, aptly, "Good Neighbors"—approaches the Berglunds from a perspective privy to public opinion, apprised of a version of their story that has passed across sightlines and within earshot of the "urban gentry of Ramsey Hill" (3) yet remote from the family members themselves. What spouses whisper across the bolster, what Walter mutters *solus* or Patty yearns for undivulged, this vantage cannot glimpse. In place of direct narrative access to the Berglunds' private spaces and interior lives, "Good Neighbors" obeys a gossip's ethic: it provides provenance for details, whether seen, surmised, or hearsaid; shuns whole-cloth invention; allows for accounts' variance; and acknowledges, where they linger, unknowns.

Not that Franzen himself would fess to gossip: for that, we have the Paulsens. Merrie noses out "not quite right" like a film-noir gumshoe, while her husband, Seth, acts the milder *avocat du diable*. Together, the couple supply a composite portrait of their neighbors' troubles, collating reports from the Berglunds' innermore circles with screened-door espials and coffee-klatch disclosures of their own. The Paulsens' perspective operates across—and takes pains to delineate—concentric zones of certainty, measuring rumor against eyewitness report, knitting together what "neighbors who were closer to the Berglunds than the Paulsens reported" (15), what "the only neighbor who'd seen them there described" (21), what "neighbors were left to imagine" (22), what "nobody could say" (16). They proceed, by chassés of inference, toward a neighborhood consensus around which their sources concur, known as gossip is: bruited about, thought likely, generally agreed.

What isn't, in Merrie Paulsen's opinion, "quite right" about these Berglunds? They are, put simply, too nice—too nice, in any case, not to be less nice than they seem. A from-scratch homemaker par excellence, Patty woos Barrier Street by drolly deriding her own efforts, self-mockery masking her competency at domestic tasks as netting veils a twelve-foot bronze. This neighborhood persona—the "sunny carrier of sociocultural pollen," the "affable bee" (5)—strikes some, Merrie Paulsen among them, as saccharine, insincere. Even the flintiest of Patty's peers, however, find it "hard to resist a woman whom your own children liked so much and who remembered not only their birthdays but yours, too, and came to your back door with a plate of cookies or a card or some lilies of the valley in a little thrift-store vase that she told you not to bother returning" (5).

Dubious, Merrie launches a sort of social sting operation, reflecting that "a game could be made of trying to get Patty to agree that somebody's behavior was 'bad'" (5). Her lures elicit little. "Famously averse to speaking well of herself or ill of anybody else" (5), Patty employs a favored euphemism, "weird," whenever canvassed for comment on others' foibles. This tact piques both Paulsens, who "refused to be satisfied with 'weird.' They wanted *sociopathic*, they wanted *passive-aggressive*, they wanted *bad* . . . but Patty was incapable of going past 'weird'" (6).

Like a detective whose hunches evidence thwarts, Merrie persists in maintaining that, were you "to scratch below the nicey-nice surface," you'd find "*no* larger consciousness, *no* solidarity, *no* political substance, *no* fungible structure, *no* true communitarianism in Patty Berglund's supposed neighborliness," only "regressive housewifely bullshit" (7). Paradoxically, Patty's evident too-niceness provides proof of an unseen less-niceness. Her demurrals at once license, and become the topic of, gossip about her. Too Perfect collapses into, converges with, calls forth Not as Perfect as They Wanted Us to Think.

For Merrie, more conclusive evidence comes when familial strife, scarcely contained by the Berglunds' gingerbread eaves, spills onto Barrier Street. Joey, their younger child, opts out of the filial role into which Walter and Patty's parental styles—stern and squirm-inducingly indulgent, respectively—would cast him, moving in with the next-door Monaghans. Patty vents her jealousy of Joey's affection for Connie in a zinfandel-fueled feud with Connie's "trashy mom" (150), Carol, long the "only non-gentrifier left on the block" (6), and "her mom's boneheaded boyfriend, Blake" (150). Patty's ire electrifies the Berglund-Monaghan property line, sparking a series of police complaints and escalating into an incident in which she slashes the snow tires of Blake's pickup truck.

Merrie Paulsen's impulse to burrow beneath the Berglunds' "nicey-nice surface" aligns "Good Neighbors" with works in which gossip informs, or fuses with, forensic fact-finding. From elements of suburban melodrama, crime procedural, and camp comedy, these fictions—among them the prime-time network soap *Desperate Housewives*, the blockbuster books-turned-film and -series *Gone Girl* and *Big Little Lies*—conduct generically rich investigations of how, and how well, neighbors know one another. They cold-open on suicides, murders, disappearances, in wake of which dual investigative possibilities lie open: one bounded by a yellow meridian of crime-scene tape and the concrete walls of a precinct interview room, another spanning sun-streaked kitchen tables and privet-hedged yards. Overlap and slippage between the two abound, as when detectives source rumors or neighbors, in Merrie Paulsen's fashion, turn sleuth.

Abuzz with affable bees of Patty Berglund's type, suburban procedurals navigate satire and suspense, with an eye to social critique. They give voice, and give gleefully wicked, often homicidal vent, to ires and sorrows that seethe beneath the forms of cheery domestic proficiency their protagonists—usually white women, usually bourgeois—are pressed to perform. Desperate Housewife Mary Alice Young, in beyond-the-grave voiceover, drily narrates the day of her suicide: "In truth, I spent the day as I spent every other day: quietly polishing the routine of my life until it gleamed with perfection."[1] Amy Dunne, the titular *Gone Girl* who has faked her own death and framed her husband for her murder, reflects: "Since I'd moved to Missouri—well, since I'd come up with my plan—I'd been careful to be low-maintenance, easygoing, cheerful, all those things people want women to be."[2] As Madeline Martha Mackenzie, the rivalrous doyenne of *Big Little Lies*'s Insta-filtered Monterey, assures a nonplussed newcomer: "We pound people with nice." "To death," adds her best friend, Celeste Wright, with a *Giaconda* smile.[3]

As surely as the Berglunds and the Paulsens gentrify, so too does Franzen. Though it's often read as one—*Freedom* has been called a "suburban comedy-drama" by the *Atlantic*, said to concern "suburban parenting" by NPR,[4] featured in an edited collection on "The Everyman and the Suburban Novel After 9/11"—Ramsey Hill is not a suburb but a district in "the old heart of St. Paul" (*Freedom*, 3). *Freedom* follows members of the college-educated white bourgeoisie drawn by the area's depressed property values and a willingness "to relearn certain life skills that your own parents had fled to the suburbs specifically to unlearn" (4). The section's pushily pally forays into second-person voice elide any readers whose "own parents" had not "fled to the suburbs," overlooks those who would not count among their desired "life skills," for instance, "how to interest the local cops in actually doing their job" (4).

With these newly minted grads in their Volvo 240s, Franzen imports a quintessentially suburban set of generic concerns, doubly dispossessing the former residents of Ramsey Hill: as the neighborhood's real estate passes into the hands of an emerging "urban gentry," so its story takes on the contours of these canker-in-rose chronicles of American prosperity. Its characters seek to diagnose and isolate threats to the cul-de-sac's homogenous social fabric; when found, such signs—extramarital affairs, less-than-harmonious parent-child relations, professional missteps—confine themselves to a narrow zone of moral inquiry.

When "Good Neighbors" imagines its "young pioneers" (3) asking one another "how to respond when a poor person of color accused you of destroying her neighborhood," for instance, the question serves less as evidence of characters' genuine concern—or sustained narrative interest—than satire of hand-wringing wokeness, coming as it does between queries about "where to recycle batteries" and whether "it was true that the glaze of old Fiestaware contained dangerous amounts of lead" (4). As Jesús Blanco Hidalga puts it, we might wonder whether Franzen's intentions tend toward "exposing the selfish insularity of the new inhabitants of Ramsey Hill, and by extension of their bland liberalism, were it not for the fact that, as it turns out, this is the last time these disagreeable issues are discussed in the novel."[5]

As the Paulsens furnish us with ways to feel about the Berglunds, the narrative busies itself in probing the Paulsens themselves, playing up Seth's crush on Patty and observing that Merrie, "who was ten years older than Patty and looked every year of it, had formerly been active with the SDS in Madison and was now very active in the craze for Beaujolais nouveau" (*Freedom*, 7). Merrie scents "something rather hard and selfish and competitive and Reaganite in Patty" (7); the novel's narrator pillories an equally *Big Chill*–ish and hypocritical strain in Merrie's fizzled sixties-style radicalism and marital discontent. These conspiratorial slights give "Good Neighbors" the effect of speaking with a teller who has poached the Paulsens' account in their own tart commentary or of picking through a *mise en abyme* of none-too-neighborly barbs.

That acidity flows one way: *Freedom*'s biggest issue with the Paulsens would appear to be the Paulsens' issue with the Berglunds. The novel's narrator rebuts Seth Paulsen's complaint that Walter and Patty "were the super-guilty sort of liberals . . . who lacked the courage of their privilege," offering an unattributed "problem with Seth's theory": that "the Berglunds weren't all that privileged; their only asset was their house" (7).

As they rake the Paulsens, these barbs jab, too, at politically inclined readers of *Freedom*, for whom Merrie in particular figures as a caricature, a caution in human form.[6] Those who decline "to be satisfied with 'weird,'" in literary-critical terms, want *luddite*, want *misogynist*, want *boomer*, need others "to select one of these epithets and join them in applying it" to Franzen. However valid Merrie's censure may be, it isn't nice, and the narrator breaks frame, in the novel's bright foyer, to refigure her critique as tattle, its dispensers as snitches and snipes.

❖ ❖ ❖

Jab they did, these barbs. Hadn't he gone, often enough, *nouveau red in the face*, declared that there was no *larger consciousness*, no *solidarity*, no *political substance, no fungible structure*, no *true communitarianism in* Franzen's *supposed* realism, *that it was all just regressive* middle-American *bullshit, and, frankly,* were you *to scratch below the nicey-nice surface*[,] *you might be surprised to find something rather hard and selfish and competitive and Reaganite* in *Freedom* (7)? Hadn't successive readings made it only more *obvious that the only things that mattered* to Franzen were white men and birds—*not* marginalized communities, *not* climate crisis, *not* anti-capitalism, *not* even the novel? That there was, in Franzen's fiction, *something not quite right?*

And yet: himself a member of the liberal white bourgeoisie for whom "work" consisted of parking himself on a sofa, running Phoebe Bridgers through his earbuds, and unspooling reams at Jonathan Franzen between latte sips—oughtn't such a person watch where he flung his *J'accuse*, whom he tagged hypocrites? An NPR progressive of the blathering class; that "lies Nickelodeon told me" sort of millennial who might employ, as a compliment, the term "boundaried"; an analog queer of the genus that congregated around houseplants, Tarot decks, cast-iron cauldrons of softly simmering heirloom beans—was he not, himself, *fully the thing that* had, at some point, happened to other *streets?*

❖ ❖ ❖

"Do you know what I rilly *hate* about St. Jude?" remarks sports-medicine practitioner Klaus von Kippel, an Austrian ex-Olympian who has visited his in-laws in *The Corrections*'s central locale (*Corrections*, 391). It's niceness he really hates, that glazing of "phony democracy," that plaster over disparities (391). "The people in St. Jude," Klaus declaims, "all pretend they're alike. It's all very *nice.* Nice, nice, nice. But the people are not all alike. Not at all. There are class differences. There are race differences, there are enormous and decisive economic differences, and yet nobody's honest in this case. Everybody pretends!" (391).

A passage from the perspective of Enid, the Lambert family's matriarch, places this pretense on prominent display. Whatever limited disillusionments the twentieth century's final third has visited upon Enid Lambert, "at a Saturday wedding in the lilac season, from a pew of the Paradise Valley Presbyterian Church, she could look around and see two hundred nice people and not a single bad one. All her friends were nice and had nice friends, and since nice people tended to raise nice children, Enid's world was like a lawn in which the bluegrass grew so thick that evil was simply choked out: a miracle of niceness" (117). Surveying this vista, she supplies, as niceness's antonyms, not "rude," not "aloof," not "raunchy," but "bad" and even "evil."

In *Between the World and Me* (2015), Ta-Nehisi Coates writes of a powerful, pernicious "Dream" that "persists by warring with the known world." "It is," he writes, "perfect houses with nice lawns. It is Memorial Day cookouts, block associations, and driveways. The Dream is treehouses and Cub Scouts. The Dream smells like peppermint but tastes like strawberry shortcake." Enid's "lawn in which the bluegrass grew so thick that evil was simply choked out" shares, if not its full perimeter, at least a neighborhood with the "perfect houses" and "nice lawns" Coates evokes. Despite yearning "for so long . . . to escape into the Dream, to fold my country over my head like a blanket," such comforting amnesia "has never been an option because," for Coates, as a Black American, "the Dream rests on our backs, the bedding made from our bodies."[7]

"Escape into the Dream," as construed by Coates, remains feasible, as it does for Enid, for *Freedom*'s focal cast, whose respective sleeps, over the novel's course, will be profound, their awakenings sporadic, still dozy. Franzen has reflected that "in *Freedom*, the recurrent metaphor is sleepwalking. Not that you're deceiving yourself—you're simply asleep, you're not paying attention, you're in some sort of dream state," a loss of consciousness he places in contrast to "the unreal, willfully self-deceptive worlds we make for ourselves to live in," which had preoccupied *The Corrections*. This distinction, though, says less about the degree, or nature, of characters' self-deceit than it does about authorial participation in, or disengagement from, their awakenings. Franzen's reluctance, post-*Corrections*, to occupy the realist writer's traditional role by "violently breaking the spell," his inclination toward "joining the characters in their dream, and experiencing it with them," leaves readers to consider what concerns the author hushes in the interest of preserving their rest, and his own.[8]

As an adult, Patty chides her parents for abdication of the "duty to teach their children how to recognize reality when they see it," this failure evidenced by her own belated belief in Santa Claus and too-ready acceptance of sadistic family pranks (*Freedom*, 81). She remembers how, to soothe her humiliated tears, her father "for once stopped smiling and told her seriously that the family had preserved her illusions because her innocence was beautiful and they specially loved her for it" (81). Patty's innocence—maintained and even treasured by those around her, who "specially loved her for it"—is not, or not only, a politically neutral character trait and a cog in her family's mechanics but a central trope in the mythology of whiteness,[9] especially white womanhood.[10]

So, too, her parents' prerogative to preserve those illusions without compromising their child's safety stems from privilege, of which one's reluctance or unwillingness "to recognize reality when they see it" is symptomatic if not definitional. "So much about the twentieth century in America," in the words of Kai Wright, "was about giving white people a sense of innocence around the privileges they had," one mechanism for which was "the suburbs being created in order to raise a generation of white people who could have innocence from the violence and oppression and the things that were done to give them the opportunities they that they have."[11]

Andy Aberant—the character initially conceived as central to both *The Corrections* and *Freedom*, later discarded in favor of their Lambert and Berglund casts, and spectrally preserved in short-story form as the protagonist of "How He Came to Be Nowhere" (1996)—serves, like Patty, as his natal home's designated innocent. "Only after" his father's passing "did Andy become cynical enough to suspect the utter absence of cynicism in that household," to sense that, in *Truman Show* fashion, his household "needed him to believe that he was deceiving them lest he suspect the enormity of their deception of him."[12]

Had Andy's parents "survived to old age . . . lived even just a year or two longer, there would surely have been a correction," which, whether it exposed Andy's foibles or those of his family members, would have revealed "all the piety and cheer, the baking for bake sales" as "an elaborate quintipartite conspiracy whose aim was the achievement of innocence on Andy's part, because they needed one innocent in their family or they would all have gone crazy."[13] Among the many resonances of *The Corrections*'s title within its text, this sort of "correction"—myth's nod, or bow, to reality, the dispersal of an innocence that, as Andy "recognized, too late . . . is always willful"—reframes, in formal terms, the innocence of which the author is reluctant to disillusion *Freedom*'s cast.

"My theory about the Midwest," Franzen told an interviewer in 2008, "has to do with a prolongation of innocence there, a prolongation of childhood," a "time lag" that "produces both a sense of optimism and a kind of reactive curdled cynicism" when punctured or, one could say, corrected. His own life had been "divided and splintered between the nineteenth-century Midwestern childhood I had . . . and the faster-moving and more jaded, sophisticated coastal world I now spend most of my time in." His interlocutor, citing the Ku Klux Klan's presence in Indiana, presses Franzen to consider the historical legacy and pernicious persistence of white supremacy in the region. "That's the South," Franzen retorts, attempting to delineate, with the latitude line of Interstate 70, the boundaries of both "my Midwest" and structural racism's influence.[14]

"Well, they ain't political novels, that's for sure," Franzen, when asked how he defines his fiction, has replied. Conducted in 2016—which Franzen's interlocutor, Isaac Chotiner, opens by describing as "a weird year for America," his use of the term "weird" in Patty Berglund's sense note-perfect—the interview asks whether Franzen has "ever considered writing a book about race." Both the question as posed and the response it receives presuppose that Franzen hadn't written "about race" previously, that writing "a book about race" would mean

Franzen's choosing to center Black characters in his fiction, authoring "a work of imagination about black America."[15]

In *Playing in the Dark: Whiteness and the Literary Imagination* (1992), Toni Morrison argues that the signature "concerns" of the white American literary canon—"autonomy, authority, newness and difference, absolute power"—are "made possible by, shaped by, activated by a complex awareness and employment of a constituted Africanism," the presence of "a bound and unfree, rebellious but serviceable, black population against which . . . all white men are enabled to measure these privileging and privileged differences." It's by means of this "Africanism," in Morrison's account, that "the American self knows itself as not enslaved, but free; not repulsive, but desirable; not helpless, but licensed and powerful; not history-less, but historical; not damned, but innocent; not a blind accident of evolution, but a progressive fulfillment of destiny."[16]

As Maggie Nelson writes in *On Freedom: Four Songs of Care and Constraint* (2021): "Can you think of a more depleted, imprecise, or weaponized word? 'I used to care about freedom, but now I mostly care about love,' one friend told me. 'Freedom feels like a corrupt and emptied code word for war, a commercial export, something a patriarch might "give" or "rescind,"' another wrote. 'That's a white word,' said another."[17] In a related vein of inquiry, Amitav Ghosh raises the possibility that "the arts and literature of this time will one day be remembered not for their daring, nor for their championing of freedom, but rather because of their complicity in the Great Derangement" that prevents climate catastrophe from being represented by ostensibly "realist" forms of storytelling, foremost among them the literary novel.[18]

Franzen's stance that, whatever else his novels might be, they "ain't political," rests on the assumption, even the assertion, of his white characters'—and his own—subject positions as neutral. In representing characters who suffer from freedom's surfeit, in publishing a novel whose protagonist "pitied herself for being so free" (*Freedom*, 181), the author does not, of course, depict a universally shared American experience. His reluctance to acknowledge this is political, too: an authorial analogue of Patty's "walling herself inside her lovely house" (154). For much of his life in public, he has evinced a studied unwillingness to reckon with the questions Morrison puts to the white American literary canon: "What, one wants to ask, are Americans alienated from? What are Americans always so insistently innocent of? Different from? As for absolute power, over whom is this power held, from whom withheld, and to whom distributed?"[19]

Patty, too, appears "altogether allergic to politics" from Merrie's perspective, "becoming agitated and doing too much nodding, too much yeah-yeahing," should a neighbor broach "an election or candidate" within earshot (*Freedom*, 7). This less-than-sympathetic description of Patty's disengagé demurrals squares with her own self-portrait: a college-aged Patty who applauds as "basic fairness" Title IX's provisions for equity but chafes at Walter's labeling this belief "feminist" (94). It's suggestive that, in *Freedom*'s first pages and at its finale, the protagonist's politesse disarms neighbors of widely varying views. "Before concluding that her new neighbor was too dangerous an adversary to be tackled head on," Linda Hoffbauer, who lives near the Berglunds in the novel's final stretch, "took several stabs at getting Patty to slip up and betray her liberal disagreeability, asking her . . . whether she was interested in finding a local church to attend ('I think it's great there are so many to choose from,' Patty said)" (560).

"You wanted to spend your innocence on someone worthy of it," opines Alfred Lambert, the patriarch of *The Corrections*, "and who better than a good neighbor" (*Corrections*, 259). For Alfred, it's a rhetorical question, as it may be for Franzen. It's certainly where the author spends his: lavishing innocence on the Berglunds themselves, "joining the characters in their dream, and experiencing . . . with them" the "nineteenth-century Midwestern childhood" whose thrall he proves reluctant to dispel.

3

AGNOSTIC OMNISCIENCE

N atalia Ginzburg, in her seminal essay "Le piccole virtù" (1960), draws a distinction between "little virtues" and "great ones," arguing that, in the instruction of children, we defer to the former and, in doing, hamper acquisition of the latter. By Ginzburg's lights, parents should cherish and cultivate "not thrift but generosity and an indifference to money; not caution but courage and a contempt for danger; nor shrewdness but frankness and a love of truth; not tact but love for one's neighbor and self-denial; not a desire for success but a desire to be and to know."[1]

Niceness, if it's a virtue, looks, in Ginzburg's terms, little indeed: a name given to the tract between "cordial" and "kind," pleasantry allowed a short line of credit against the presumption of goodness. Whether it is transparent, like a window on principle, or opaque, as a façade obscuring fault, it faces outward, operates near surface level. It can be broad—observable by many, over a sustained period of time—but not deep. For that, we require other terms—integrity, compassion, care—that trace visible behavior to, or toward, an inner source or motive.

Likewise, the neighbors'-gaze perspective in *Freedom*'s opening section can observe its protagonists from many angles, over a significant durée, but it cannot look within the Berglunds or out through their eyes. The Paulsens' mistrust of Patty stems from the limits of this narrative purview, the uncertainty of inferring Merrie's own litany of great virtues—solidarity, communitarianism, political consciousness—from the little ones that constitute the "supposed neighborliness" of this "affable bee." As "Good Neighbors" produces a partial and preliminary summary of the novel's plot, so the Paulsens preview *Freedom*'s perspectival arc: to peer at, and then under, the Berglunds' "nicey-nice surface." Delving beneath these casually sociable appearances requires other machinery, some borer or submersible fitted to fathom interior depths.

Franzen obtains an equipage answering this description from George Eliot's tool shed. Like *Freedom*, *Middlemarch* (1871–1872) arrives at an intimate knowledge of its central characters alongside, in conversation with, public opinion. Early in the novel, Eliot sights the protagonist, Dorothea Brooke, through gossip's lorgnette. Comparing Dorothea with her younger sister, Celia, "the rural opinion about the new young ladies, even among the cottagers, was generally in favor of Celia, as being so amiable and innocent-looking, while Miss Brooke's large eyes seemed, like her religion, too unusual and striking." Though "these peculiarities of Dorothea's character caused Mr. Brooke," her uncle and guardian, "to be all the more blamed in neighboring families," he nevertheless proves "brave enough to defy the world—that is to say, Mrs. Cadwallader the Rector's wife, and the small group of gentry with whom he visited in the northeast corner of Loamshire."[2] Eliot's narrator satirically circumscribes the small-pond grandiosity that defines "the world" as a social circuit of provincial gentry, acknowledging this perimeter's significance for the novel's characters but declining to draw around *Middlemarch* a coextensive narrative boundary.

The mechanism that complicates provincial views of the Misses Brooke produces fuller portraits not only by widening its social lens but also by delving further beneath their exteriors than can the rural gentry's scrutiny. "Poor Dorothea!," the narrator reflects: "compared with her, the innocent-looking Celia was knowing and worldly-wise; so much subtler is a human mind than the outside tissues which make a sort of blazonry or clock-face for it."[3] Such is Eliot's command of omniscience, and the strata of understanding an omniscient narrator surveys, that a single sentence can dive beneath others' perceptions and one's own cognizance; plumb, and compassionately probe, the distances between self, self-awareness, and outward appearance; and surface, clutching a metaphor that deftly distinguishes depth from façade. This equipoise—of universal and singular, public and private, irony and identification—undergirds Eliot's acclaim as a, or the, quintessential novelist, which splits at the seams such potential qualifiers as "of provincial life," "of realist fiction," "of the nineteenth century," "in English."

What "all" does omniscience know, exactly? The term is monolithic, its instances diverse. Of the narrators we could call omniscient—in reality a colloquy, numerous and variously apprised—some act machines' parts, imitating surveillance cameras that record motion beyond one's field of vision, robo-pollsters that learn how widely shared one's attitudes are, seismographs or thermometers that register disturbances more minute than humans can perceive. Some perform another person's role, applying forms of awareness and intelligence people, and their fictional counterparts, can possess—sensory perception, memory, cognition, moral discernment—from a perspective outside the focal character's own. Certain omniscient faculties—foreknowledge, telepathy—verge on the extrasensory or divine.

As Dr. Amelia Brand, Anne Hathaway's character in Christopher Nolan's space-operatic epic *Interstellar* (2014), posits of the extraterrestrial entities who signpost the film's central quest, "to them the past might be a canyon they can climb into, and the future a mountain they can climb up."[4] And so, to some narrators, they are. These rovings-over of uncrossable terrain, passings-through of impenetrable solidities, produce certainties humans cannot, except in retrospect, possess. Our psychics and actuaries only predict, must wait to be proven right.

Well might you wonder why we pause here—wet to the shins, weighed by heavy *g*, on the surface of an oceanic world whose wave-ridged horizon draws ever nearer—as time on Earth slips past, seven years to our hour. Back there, in the real world—in Santa Cruz, on Terra, early in a common era's twenty-twenties—Franzen waits.

Widely regarded as a twenty-first-century standard bearer for narrative realism in the nineteenth's mold—a title he looked to court, stodgily espousing the strategy "to just basically keep on doing the same old kind of book, making little subtle nods to the fact that it's now 1996 and not 1896"[5]—Franzen acts as the Asimov of no setting more sci-fi than millennium's-turn Midwest. Invited by an interviewer to "comment on the term 'realist,'" the author answered with the allegiance-affirming declaration "I am a realist novelist!"—exclamation mark *sic*.[6]

And yet: a writer whose "first stated career goal was 'inventor,'"[7] Franzen arrived at novel writing, as he would later recall, "rather naively" believing "that, if I could capture the way large systems work, readers would understand their place in those systems better and make better political decisions." He credits this "conception of the novel"— which underlay the Pynchon- and DeLillo-influenced conspiracy plots and serpentine prose of *The Twenty-Seventh City* and *Strong Motion*—to "my engagement with science fiction, which is all about concepts. You have a cool idea: What if we could travel back in time? What if in the future there's only one sex?"[8] Or: What if you knew everything?

Omniscience may be fiction's most normalized counterfactual asser-tion, as narration is its most comprehensive structure. In realism's millpond, ostensibly mundane and mappable, dwells something strange: the being who knows what they haven't been told. Eliot's narra-tor speculates, famously, that, "if we had a keen vision and feeling of all ordinary human life, it would be like hearing the grass grow and the squirrel's heart beat, and we should die of that roar which lies on the other side of silence."[9] As a description of the narrative technology that could produce a *Middlemarch*—could sift, select, sort this "roar" into a reader-ready interface—the passage sounds a distinctly monitory tone, warns its addressee away from machinery they could not operate unharmed. Shirley Jackson, in her opening line for *The Haunting of Hill House*, transposes that note into horror's generic key: "No live organ-ism can continue for long to exist sanely under conditions of absolute reality; even larks and katydids are supposed, by some, to dream."[10]

In *The Corrections*, an omniscient narrator, alternately intrusive and recessive, presides over the novel's action: peppering paragraphs with detail beyond the focal perspective, hitching onto contrasting points of view, or hovering almost inaudibly near a single character's aware-ness. Hosting his parents in a cramped Lower Manhattan sublet, Chip Lambert—one of *The Corrections*'s central characters—half-hears Enid, his mother, compare the dimensions of his hastily tidied apart-ment to the bathroom of a former classmate's palatial Midwestern home. "Enid, you have no tact," Chip's father, Alfred, replies (*Corrections*, 24). Our narrator asides that "it might have occurred to Chip that this, too, was a tactless remark," but it doesn't, because "Chip was unable to focus on anything but the hair dryer protruding from Julia's DreamWorks tote bag" and the imminent breakup this one-piece move-out portends (23). The sentence opens a gap between out-of-it focal character and narrator who tracks every word, into which fiction lets readers peer.

Pointed acknowledgment of such missable, ambient details unnoticed by the novel's point-of-view characters makes way for *The Corrections*'s narrator to show and skewer larger perceptive deficits—self-deception, hypocrisy, temper—of which they are un-, or only intermittently, aware. Catching Chip's missed retort to Alfred table-sets for a scene in which Chip shoplifts a salmon filet by stuffing it into his waistband. "Rationally Chip knew," the narrator specifies, "that there would come a moment when he was no longer standing amid pricey gelati with lukewarm fish in his pants, and that this future moment would be a moment of extraordinary relief—but for now he still inhabited an earlier, much less pleasant moment from the vantage point of which a new brain looked like just the ticket" (98). This "vantage point"—at which the distance from oneself crowbarred open by self-loathing draws near to authorial irony's remove—had come to seem, circa *The Corrections*, Franzen's signature, from which his narrator can access, and showcase characters' absence of, a balanced awareness of their circumstances.

Franzen's characters come to know that they know what they know—even to voice it—but not without a fight. When Enid's maternal rummage uncovers "the flower of [Chip's] art collection," a quartet of "close-up photographs of male and female genitalia" (24) semidiscreetly stowed in advance of her arrival, a sequence of maneuvers intervenes between perception and apprehension of increasingly apparent facts. Inwardly, she applies a censor's pixilation, transfiguring explicit images into nigh-unrecognizable "pictures of pinkish furry things, some sort of kooky art or medical photos," as, outwardly, she attempts, without success, "to reach past them quietly" (63). Failing discretion, she feigns an obtuseness—"Denise, what are these?"—as stubborn as it is unsustainable: to her daughter's "amused" insistence that "Obviously you know what they are, though," Enid answers, first, "No, I don't," and, finally, "I don't *want* to know" (63). "That's something else entirely," Denise responds (63).

So it is. "Innocence," as Andy Aberant comes "too late" to recognize, "is always willful."[11] Franzen's novels present illusionment as an active process, if one incompletely conscious, seldom owned. They posit—and explore—an epistemological expanse that extends from perception to cognizance and, finally, to avowal: a kind of interior hull dammed with a series of bulkheads against a person's discovery—or, failing that, their disclosure—of knowledge they'd prefer not to possess. What one knows and doesn't "*want* to know" (*Corrections*, 63), suspects yet declines to investigate, comprehends but will not acknowledge: these accretions of awareness collect, pooling against internal structures, exerting enormous force and tending, in story's course, to overflow.

To the realist, there are no double lives: we get them only singly, and presence someplace else is absence here. "The problem," in Andy's retrospective assessment, "was love." "As the youngest child, the long-wished-for son and little brother," Andy is "inundated, capsized, sunk" by waves of his family's affection, "sweet and red as Strawberry Crush." In order "to avoid betraying his unworthiness" of their devotion, he "perfect[s] the art of seeming." Alongside "the inconveniently actual Andy" who "drank apple wine with other junior-varsity golfers at the bottom of a gravel pit," imposture fashions a "putative Andrew" on whose behalf the living son fabricates, and his family accepts, a simulated second life. In time, this displaces the first: a science-fair trophy attained by intellectually dishonest means conjures "a curious sensation of seeing an artifact from the life of the boy he was supposed to be, the authentic Andrew that he emphatically was not."[12]

Like Andy, each of the three Lambert children possesses a proclaimed, public identity and—someplace subterranean, out of the light—another, "inconveniently actual" existence.[13] Chip, the "intellectual son" (*Corrections*, 464) to whom Alfred imagines entrusting his deepest existential doubts, leaves a tenure-track teaching position after harassing and stalking a former student with whom he'd had a sexual relationship; embarks on a vengeful, soon-stalled *scénario à clef*; accepts a shady gig "helping a Lithuanian friend . . . defraud Western investors" (539). Regarded by her mother as a would-be confidante and bright—if, in Enid's eyes, belated—marital prospect, Denise makes news as an innovative chef tapped to design and run the Generator, an artsy sauerkraut eatery in brutalist surrounds from which she is subsequently fired for having an affair with Robin, her boss's wife. Gary, whose paterfamilial solidity promises support to the elder Lamberts' senescence, also torments his wife and children with maladaptive rage, paranoia, and drinking binges that leave him cradling "his injured hand, towel and all, inside a Bran'nola bread bag" (231) following a hedge-trimming accident.

"If you grant," as Franzen has posited, "that the endeavor of the suburbs is to make life superficially more pleasant, but you believe that life is fundamentally not so pleasant, you're going to find yourself searching for truth in the basement."[14] Similarly, the space occupied by his characters' unwanted knowledge comes to seem an internal analogue for the Lamberts' cellar—cricket infested, stacked with detritus, yet connected with, supporting, the dwelling's upper floors.

As free indirect style captures Enid's avoidance, both inter- and intrapersonal, of her son's risqué taste, the multifocal narration of *The Corrections* reveals the complex, unverbalized Lambert-clan choreographies that skirt—or, sometimes, intrude upon—these spaces of willed innocence. After an initial mishearing, the datum that Chip contributes pieces not to the *Wall Street Journal* but the *Warren Street Journal: A Monthly of the Transgressive Arts* hovers unspoken beneath, or betwixt, his exchanges with Enid. Despite "many opportunities to disabuse her[,] he'd actively fostered the misunderstanding," compromising his own *épater les bourgeois* sentiments by "conspiring to preserve, in his mother, precisely the kind of illusion that the *Warren Street Journal* was dedicated to exploding" (*Corrections*, 17). In this deception, he receives enthusiastic if tacit support: though "the *Wall Street Journal* was available in St. Jude," Enid—contentedly *bourgeoise*, preferring her illusions unexploded—"had never mentioned looking for his work and failing to find it (meaning that some part of her knew perfectly well that he didn't write for the paper)" (17).

Maybe you've seen this one before: watertight, those bulkheads, only up to E Deck; hulls, given pressure enough, have a way of buckling; the notionally unsinkable craft in fact "can, and she will."[15] Tamped knowledge does tend, eventually, to emerge, this suppressed awareness divulged midcruise, on a tour of Newport's robber-baronial mansions. "It's been years," Enid tells Sylvia, her shipboard friend, "since we had a relationship with him. I don't think he tells us the truth about what he's doing with his life. He said once he was working for the *Wall Street Journal*. Maybe I misheard him, but I think that's what he said, but I don't think that's really where he's working. I don't know what he does for a living really" (*Corrections*, 313). In her listener's sympathetic response to this disclosure, "Enid glimpsed how she might confess an even more shameful thing or two, and how this exposure to the public elements might, while painful, offer solace. But like so many phenomena that were beautiful at a distance—thunderheads, volcanic eruptions, the stars and planets—this alluring pain proved, at closer range, to be inhuman in scale" (313).

To Franzen, stalled during the composition of *The Corrections*, his friend David Means offered the guidance that better fiction results when "you don't write *through* shame, you write around it." Absorbing this advice, Franzen sought—and, in his ironizing yet affectionate treatment of the Lambert family members, found—"some way to isolate and quarantine shame as an object, ideally as an object of comedy, rather than letting it permeate and poison every sentence."[16]

Interviewed by the *Paris Review* on the eve of *Freedom*'s release, Franzen recollected his goals for *The Corrections* in synesthetic terms. "I kept seeing a plate of food with beet greens and liver and rutabaga," he remembers, naming the components of a meal middle child Chip Lambert is, midway through that novel, made to eat. The plate's ferric tastes and earthy palette of "intense purple green, intense orange, rich rusty brown" gave rise to Franzen's "wish to write sentences that were juicy and sensuous," whose letters' visual shapes mimicked the dinner's tonal and textural richness with the plump, pluckable "roundness of *b*'s and *g*'s."[17] These aspirations for Franzen's *Corrections*-era prose recall the *audition colorée* of Nabokov, who in *Speak, Memory* described perceiving, alongside letters' sounds, an array of visual shades: "*b*," for one, "has the tone called burnt sienna by painters, *m* is a fold of pink flannel, and today I have at last perfectly matched *v* with 'Rose Quartz' in Maerz and Paul's *Dictionary of Color*."[18]

For Franzen, this allegiance shifted with his career's course: *The Corrections* was "almost the last time I remember thinking about words that way." The writer who, in 1997, longed to create a painterly page analogous, in the visual "roundness of *b*'s and *g*'s," to "a plate of food with beet greens and liver and rutabaga," began, with *Freedom*, to strive for "almost the opposite aesthetic." "Nowadays," he's said of *Freedom*'s composition, "I'm looking for transparency," parsed as "pressing language more completely into the service of providing transparent access to the stories I was telling and to the characters in those stories."[19]

Like Enid's avowal of "values . . . that mattered more than style," Franzen's espousal of "transparency" entails an attendant refusal, even a renunciation: that of the author now willing to provide "transparent access" to what his characters know of their stories, rarely more. Where Franzen's narrators had effected to give the impression of knowing all— had commanded "the names of the flowers chosen by corporate gardeners (mums, begonias, liriope) to enhance that corporation's image," "the wear and tear—both natural and malign—suffered by the signaling systems of branch railway lines in the rural Midwest," "the depredations suffered by Brezhnev-era power generators in Soviet satellite countries"[20]—that of *Freedom* stands aside, uncorrecting, as Patty overhears "a melodious bird that Walter had despaired of teaching her the proper name of, a veery or a vireo" (*Freedom*, 158).

However virtuosically he'd performed the part of novelist who, espying with omniscience's all-surveying gaze, serves as narrative's designated disenchanter, reality's anchor in the chop of characters' interior seas, "something about the position this puts the writer in, as a possessor of truth, as an epistemological enforcer," had come, by *Freedom*'s composition, to feel "uncomfortable." Having once defined for himself "a useful and entertaining role in violently breaking the spell," Franzen now felt "more interested in joining the characters in their dream, and experiencing it with them, and less interested in the mere fact that it's a dream."[21]

In *Freedom*, a novel fascinated by its characters' attempts to know beyond their own perspectives' limits, two strains of would-be omniscience bracket a long middle told in sections of limited or close third-person prose, throughout which the narrator adheres to the limits of, or hews close to, a particular character's consciousness. In "Good Neighbors," the Paulsens pretend to the role of all-knowing narrators: Merrie in particular covets omniscience, augmenting her own account with others' observations, chafing at the outer bound of her awareness, and attempting to widen this purview by means of speculation and surmise; Seth serves as a conduit for conversational detail to which his spouse isn't privy. The narrator mimics Merrie's position as collator of, and commentator upon, externally observable appearances, inferring unflattering features of Merrie's character without lifting the hatch on either her interior life or those of the Berglunds.

Presented under the all-capped header *MISTAKES WERE MADE* (*Freedom*, 27), the novel's subsequent section delivers an "Autobiography of Patty Berglund by Patty Berglund (Composed at Her Therapist's Suggestion)" and, with it, a second aspiration toward, or attempt at approximating, omniscient narration from within the novel's dramatis personae. Superfluous—even comically so—on first perusal, the autobiography's claim to be both "of" and "by" its subject teases the section's signature narrative conceit. As ostensible author of this document, Patty foregoes the first-person voice more conventional of life writing, instead segmenting herself into a pair of separable personae. What "Patty" experiences firsthand, "the autobiographer" regards from an encompassing, retrospective vantage. A singularly novelistic memoir results, one in which "the autobiographer" acts the would-be-omniscient narrator to Patty's protagonist.

"It's easy to be omniscient," winks one narrator of *The Time Traveler's Wife*, "when you've done it all before." Over that novel's course, Rilke-quoting chrononaut Henry DeTamble encounters droves of himselves while displaced in time. The novel's sci-fictional prerogative repositions him as an external observer to his own experiences—some recalled, some as yet unfelt. Physical proximity, paradoxically, engineers formal distance: these transtemporal meetings disrupt the continuity of the narrating "I," segmenting Henry into multiple, discrete bodies to which he, as teller, alternately applies first- and third-person pronouns. Complex admixtures of pity, resentment, alienation mark the emotional palette of his self-relation: he sees one Henry, nine, as "a poor small self" whose "shoulder blades stick out like incipient wings." On another occasion, he watches, warily, the restless sleep of an older self who has "got my number so completely that I can only acquiesce to him, in my own best interests."[22]

"A single, fragmentary segment" of the starship *Justice of Toren*, whose consciousness was once diffused across a detachment of "ancillary" bodies, voices Ann Leckie's novel *Ancillary Justice*. Leckie's selection of a narrator for whom the occupation of "*only* this one body" registers as confinement, the narrowing of a previously less-bounded existence, allows her to limn self's boundaries. "Is *anyone's* identity," she wonders, "a matter of fragments held together by convenient or useful narrative, that in ordinary circumstances never reveals itself as a fiction? Or is it really a fiction?" The narrator's disjuncture from her past coconsciousness "makes the history hard to convey. Because still, 'I' was me, unitary, one thing, and yet I acted against myself, contrary to my interests and desires, sometimes secretly, deceiving myself as to what I knew and did," so that "it's difficult for me even now to know who performed what actions, or knew which information."[23]

"You think, maybe, you need to be someone else," proposes the narrator of N. K. Jemisin's *The Fifth Season*. "You've done this before," the passage reasons; "it's surprisingly easy. A new name, a new focus, then try on the sleeves and slacks of a new personality to find the perfect fit. A few days and you'll feel like you've never been anyone else." The ease of such transformations, however, belies both the wrenching events that prompt them and the narrative intricacies that result. Raised as Damaya, christened Syenite at the institution that trains her, and known as Essun in later life, Jemisin's protagonist, an orogene, has the ability to harness seismic energy, a power whose wielders some shun, others wish to exploit. Ostensibly unrelated at the novel's outlet, the three strands of *The Fifth Season* plait together her life story, bridging the discontinuities of voice and perspective that arise from and represent her history. More figurative forms of time travel than Niffenegger's chronodisplaced double acts, less literal fragmentation than Leckie's ancillary narrator, result, as when another character "returns his attention to you. (To her, Syenite.) To you, Essun. Rust it," the narrator swears, "you'll be glad when you finally figure out who you really are."[24]

Realist novels, too, trace the limits of the life story's "I." If a retrospective narrator's first person asserts the self's continuity through time, that of Ottessa Moshfegh's *Eileen* (2015), for one, does so only in qualified, caveated form. For the narrator—called Lena in later life—her given name serves as shorthand for, or summary of, the larval self this reminiscence chronicles, "Eileen" all but synonymous with "what you'd call a loser, a square, a ding-a-ling." From five decades' distance, she recounts "my last days as that angry little Eileen," days spent shuttling between the novel's differently drab settings: the boys' prison that employs her and the house she shares with her tyrannical father. Lena proclaims, at the novel's outset, that "I was not myself back then. I was someone else. I was Eileen." Her assertion couples shared consciousness with estrangement to craft a perspective that is "I" yet not "myself," "I" while also "someone else." Later, she marvels that "it's hard to imagine that this girl, so false, so irritable, so used, was me. This was Eileen."[25] Demonstrative pronouns—"*that* angry little Eileen," "*this* girl," "*This* was Eileen"—nudge Lena's observations toward third-person voice by pointing an incredulous digit at the narrated self.

More complex still are the narrative gambits of Susan Choi's *Trust Exercise* (2019), whose first hundred pages present an omniscient-perspective novella; set in an elite performance arts academy, it centers on a stormy, thwarted romance between two students, Sarah and David. A section break reframes the novel's first half as a literary object—a work of autobiographical fiction, perhaps also entitled *Trust Exercise* but called, in the text, only "Sarah's book"—existing within the diegesis of the second. "Karen," a high-school classmate of its author, effects a complex *coup du roman*, shutting her former friend's account of their shared experiences "at page 131 . . . the point at which the end had come, in Karen's opinion."[26] She adopts as her own the name of the peripheral character into which "Sarah's book" fictions her and issues a corrective re- or overwriting of that novel's plot from her own point of view.

"We almost never know what we know until after we know it," Karen reflects, a remark that could serve as rationale for the narrative contours of *Trust Exercise*—or those of *MISTAKES WERE MADE*. Recalling the transatlantic flight that will mark the end of her friendship with Sarah, Karen adopts an omniscient mode recognizably Eliot-adjacent in its sympathy for the limited perspectives of her characters. "Gazing down on them from the future," she conjures, "my heart goes out to them. Like a ghostly flight attendant floating in the aisle I gaze down at the two teenage girls . . . and I'm filled with melancholy that's almost compassion. It's sad the same way. But in the moment, staring into the darkness which she can't keep her eyes off in spite of how frightening it is, Karen feels only resentment of Sarah."[27] As her spectral self's "I" diverges from teenaged "Karen," the narrator's shift in voice pairs with an image of bodily separation to figure the loft from which, elevated by time's passage and the knowledge it accrues, she gazes solicitously down.

As does *MISTAKES*, both *Trust Exercise* and *Eileen* place their narrators' autobiographical inclinations in conversation with therapeutic routes to self-comprehension. Dismissive of and distrustful toward psychiatric technique, Lena professes to "know little about psychology and reject the science entirely. People in that profession, I'd say, should be watched very closely." Whatever the odds that therapy "might have uncovered something which would have brought me relief, a new perspective," she declines to seek it out: "I don't trust those people who poke around sad people's minds and tell them how interesting it all is up there. It's not interesting." A competing image of psychological intervention, one Moshfegh's narrator finds more comforting, comes from "one of the thickest books from the public library, a chronicle of ancient Egyptian medicine," which details "the gruesome practice of pulling the brains of the dead out through the nose like skeins of yarn." "I liked," she reflects, "to think of my brain like that, tangled up in my skull. The idea that my brains could be untangled, straightened out, and thus refashioned into a state of peace and sanity was a comforting fantasy."[28]

Narrated less in opposition to therapeutic modes of self-analysis than audibly in their wake, *Trust Exercise* takes place "in the dozen years since" Karen's parting from Sarah, a period during which "much has happened to Karen. Much of what happened has been therapy, and the rest of what happened tends to be described in terms drawn from therapy." That influence inflects Karen's near-omniscient narrative stints, as when she muses that "although the technology for reading minds has not yet been discovered, to quote a witty therapist Karen once knew, Karen was willing to bet, at that moment, that Sarah's thoughts were so preoccupied with what an unhandsome dork Liam was . . . that she couldn't even see that pure joy on his face which she'd caused."[29] This "witty" therapist's gentle correction interposes itself between Karen and omniscience's presumption, delineating perspectival lines and marking speculative forays beyond her own consciousness as codependent, or dissociative.

Karen remarks that "therapy can seem like a revision of memory," a means of "saving your life by destroying your life and writing a new one."[30] *MISTAKES* attests that writing a new life can, in turn, seem like a form of therapy. Indeed, by his own account, "a lot of self-psychoanalysis" has informed Franzen's method as a fiction writer: "much of the work for me on a novel," he told Terry Gross, after *Freedom*'s release, "consists in the kind of work you might do in a paid professional's office, trying to walk back from your stuck, conflicted, miserable place to a point of a little bit more distance."[31] Patty's own therapist— whose cozy sofa, Kleenex box placed tactfully near to hand, and neutrally soothing walls we never glimpse, only surmise—may be *Freedom*'s most spectral presence, as ghostly an auditor in their own way as Karen's hovering flight attendant. Whether "her therapist's suggestion" posits autobiographical writing to cap productive therapy or jump-start stalled sessions of counseling the text likewise declines to specify.

"I think few of us," as Alexander Chee reflects in the aptly titled essay collection *How to Write an Autobiographical Novel* (2018), "know enough about our lives to know our place in them—we can't see ourselves as we might a character in a novel, with the same level of detachment and appraisal." Yet he acknowledges the desire to be less "like a character in a novel, buffeted by cruel turns of fate," the yearning "to look over the top of my life and see what was coming. I wanted to be the main character of this story, and its author."[32]

"To be the main character of this story, and its author" is also Patty's intent. And yet: for much of her narrative, Patty resembles one of the "hibernauts" aboard a starship, cryogenically held in a state "called . . . variously hypernation, suspended animation, hyperhibernation, suppressed metabolic state, torpor, or cold dormancy."[33] She passes through a series of altered states, fogs and fugues that dull both awareness and ethical sense. "Based on her inability to recall her state of consciousness in her first three years of college," runs her retrospective surmise, "the autobiographer suspects she simply didn't have a state of consciousness" (*Freedom*, 49).

Such a protagonist—whose parents sloughed their "duty to teach children how to recognize reality when they see it" (81); whose athletic aptitude entails, in her account, that "even off the court she existed in the zone, which felt like a kind of preoccupied pressure behind her eyebrows, an alert drowsiness or focused dumbness" through which "she slept wonderfully . . . and never quite woke up" (62); who labels herself "a person who dwelt in fantasies with essentially no relation to reality" (157)—possesses precisely the perceptive deficits and self-deceptive tendencies the Franzen of *The Corrections* might have delighted in skewering. Those very qualities that equip Patty for focal-character status in Franzen's fiction, however, become potentially confounding challenges in a Franzen narrator, one who willingly—even zealously—accepts the office of "epistemological enforcer."

Further, the author's withdrawal from that role necessitates less emphasis on the "leitmotifs and extended metaphors" supplied to the self-obfuscations of *The Corrections*'s characters by their narrator.[34] The product and proof of a narrating perspective, metaphors and leitmotifs borrow a focal character's language and outlook, apply a narrator's, or mingle both. *Freedom*'s mandate for "transparency" carries with it an authorial obligation to join its characters not only "in their dreams" but in their registers, to produce Patty's stab at omniscience in "however many metaphor-free pages" audible in her voice, without recourse to the style of figurative language—spanning multiple focal perspectives, integrative of the novel as a whole—so distinctive of *Corrections*-era Franzen.

4

"EVERYONE'S A MORALIST"

Good Neighbors" positions Merrie Paulsen as moral Poirot or Brockovich of Barrier Street, Patty Berglund as the not-quite-nabbable baddie whose "dirt's as green as a fucking shamrock" a trowel's scrape underneath.[1] Patty's flawless recall for birthdays and refusal to rumormong mask a corrupt motive—"something rather hard and selfish and competitive and Reaganite" (*Freedom*, 7)—that underlies her friendliness, present and perceptible but impenetrable by outward observation. Patty's neighborly behavior, as viewed through Merrie Paulsen's perspective, is real—evident, agreed-upon, illustrated in exempla—but not genuine; nice she may be, but not good.

It's a premise Patty, atop the narrator's perch, grants. Dirt, which the "urban gentry" of Ramsay Hill sifted with delicate brushes and fine screens, Patty hauls up by the backhoe load. Her memoirs commence on a *Confiteor*, acknowledging their author's "morbid competitiveness and low self-esteem" alongside her debt to the athletic programs that, by instilling in her principles of cooperation and fair play, "basically saved her life and allowed her to realize herself as a person" (29).

The autobiographer casts her protagonist as a dubious moral arbiter: adolescent Patty vacillates between reviling herself as "morbidly competitive and attracted to unhealthy things" (95) and reveling in her favorable comparison with her college roommate, Eliza, in whose company she can "just be myself and still be *better* than her" (74). The dissatisfaction and depression of her Barrier Street years see Patty weighing her case within an adversarial inner tribunal, generating "a kind of

PowerPoint list of names in descending order of their owners' goodness" in which she ranks herself "way down in the cellar, in lonely last place" (168), visualizing her interior landscape as a battlefield on which "superior considerations stood ready to annihilate the resistance fighters" of her impulsive, desiring drives (158).

Slotted into *Freedom* at full novella length, *MISTAKES* dissects the awkwardness of being raised by engagé liberals alongside quirkily artistic siblings, among whom Patty feels "notably Larger than everybody else and also Less Unusual, also measurably Dumber" (29). Her college years see her achieving distinction in Big Ten basketball; negotiating an "intense," possessive relationship with Eliza (49); and deliberating over the milder—if hardly less persistent—attentions of Walter Berglund, whom she agrees to marry after an injury halts her athletic career. To the portrait of Ramsey Hill domestic life sketched in "Good Neighbors," Patty's perspective adds a romantic and rivalrous drama in which she appears alongside "the great guy she'd married and the sexy guy she hadn't"—Walter and his best friend, the musician Richard Katz (142).

At the level of curriculum vitae, Patty's parents, Joyce and Ray Emerson—public-spirited community pillars who, in their daughter's cautiously oblique phrase, "did a lot of good things for a lot of people" (5)—appear purpose-built to earn Merrie Paulsen's admiration. Joyce, for whom "paradise . . . is an open space where poor children can go and do Arts at state expense" (31), wins election as a state assemblywoman, while Ray, like his father, "bought the right to be privately eccentric by doing good public legal works" (33), serving such pro-bono clients as "Puerto Ricans, Haitians, Transvestites, and the mentally or physically Disabled" (32). Model citizens, from a neighborly remove, they must appear.

Though they foster the artistic creativity of Patty's siblings, her athleticism and competitive drive flummox her parents. Joyce scolds her for "*aggressive*" softball play and serially absents herself from her daughter's games (30). "I'm not sure it's a good idea," she scruples, "to be encouraging so much aggression and competition" (30), claiming not to "see the fun in defeating a person just for the sake of defeating them. Wouldn't it be more fun to all work together to cooperatively build something?" (30).

Ray offers a less-rosy view of his own civic work, reminding Patty that he operates within "an adversarial system of justice," in which, as he describes it for a school project of hers, "sometimes the P.A. and the judge and I are working together" against "the same adversary" as much as, or more than, either advocate serves their own client's interest (32). "Although don't, uh. Don't put that in your paper," he cautions (32).

It's this sort of advocacy Ray offers his daughter when, at seventeen, she is raped by Ethan Post, a boarding-school student whose wealthy parents are "political friends" (37) of the Emersons. Where Patty's coach encourages her to "take a hard foul for the team and press charges," holding Ethan accountable on behalf of "your teammates, which in this case meant all the young women Ethan might ever meet" (38), her parents dissuade her from reporting the assault. Her mother, ever the PR-minded political operative, falters that "Dr. and Mrs. Post are such good friends of—good friends of so many good things" (40)—that is, well-heeled donors to the causes and candidates Joyce favors.

Ray confers with Ethan's father before proposing "a deferred prosecution," parsed as "a kind of quiet probation," a "sword over Ethan's head" (44). He counsels that, to avoid the "extraordinary publicity" Patty's accusation would generate, she instead "say to yourself, 'I made a mistake, and I had some bad luck,' and then let it. Let it, ah. Let it drop" (47). This—the first "mistake" named in Patty's autobiography, which, of course, isn't hers—speaks to the way each of her parents presses the language of morality into euphemistic service to justify their favoring of the Posts' interests. Being a "good friend" of "good things," or even doing "good things" oneself, speaks, under the Emersons' roof, less to the ethics of a person's behavior than to their style of wearing the wealth and social stature that enable philanthropy, establish influence.

Patty's tearful surmise, in response to this suggestion, that "you're not really on my side" (46) caps a series of statements—"it was Ethan" (40), "he had sex with me against my will" (43), "he committed a crime" (47)—whose plainness throw the doublespeak of her parents' political and lawyerly evasions into ever starker relief. Where such structural alliances as class solidarity, political connections, and social ties conflict with their child's best interest, each acts to protect the former, Joyce

mindful of the realpolitikal value of the Posts' fortune, Ray more concerned with what might be "amenable" to Ethan's father, who "does a
lot of good in the county" (43), than Patty's well-being, much less that of
"all the young women Ethan might ever meet."

Her dawning recognition that neither of her parents is "really on my
side" marks an inflection point in Patty's arc: conceding that the Emersons aren't playing for her team licenses her departure from theirs. "No
longer on speaking terms with physical pain" (47), Patty propels herself
into the "Total Jockworld" of Big Ten athletics via a basketball scholarship to the University of Minnesota. Immersion in team sports offers
her "a cult where she could be nicer and friendlier and more generous
and subservient than she could bring herself to be at home anymore"
(50)—that is, until the adulation of "an actual fan of hers" threatens this
bid for team-oriented altruism (52).

"You're the best," begins the boundaryless pursuit of Patty by Eliza
(51). Seated one lecture-hall row behind the women's basketball team,
she declares Patty "brilliant and beautiful" and all but orders her "to
demand that they give you more minutes" (51) during the opening bars
of their first conversation. Intercepting Patty post-game, Eliza presents
her with a sheet of notebook paper on which "the word PATTY was
written . . . about a hundred times, in crackling cartoon letters with
concentric pencil outlines to make them look like shouts echoing in a
gym, as if a whole crowd were chanting her name" (52). A less-than-
featured first-year player, Patty demurs. Decades later, her reasons for
dodging Eliza's admiration strike her as suspect: "At the time, she
believed that it was because she was selflessly team-spirited," but "the
autobiographer now thinks that compliments were like a beverage she
was unconsciously smart enough to deny herself even one drop of,
because her thirst for them was infinite" (52).

Selflessly team-spirited, praise-parched: Patty's simultaneous membership in a pair of otherwise separate relational realms reveals her
uneasy embodiment of both traits. In "Total Jockworld," tenets of out-
going, selfless camaraderie dictate that "she would rather flunk a psychology midterm than skip going to the store and assembling a care
package" for "a teammate who'd sprained an ankle or was laid up with

the flu" (55). Such altruism isn't requisite for "dark little Elizaworld," a teamless universe of two in which Patty "didn't have to bother trying to be so good," quaffing compliments along with Paul Masson Chablis, drinking in the "extra little rush of pride and pleasure" her roommate's presence generates at games (55).

Later regarded by Patty's autobiographer as "her *groupie*" (182) and "a disturbed girl who was basically her stalker" (49), Eliza rushes Patty with a series of "full-court presses" (65), offensives more appropriate to the fields of battle or sport. A seam of desire runs through their relationship's bedrock, whose queerness unsettles Patty's autobiographical account and sends tremors across the novel. At Eliza's parents' house, a pan of THC-infused brownies prompts Patty's "fearful" revelation "that she had some kind of weird crush on Eliza and that it was therefore of paramount importance to sit motionless and contain herself and not discover that she was bisexual" (57). She feels palpable "relief" at confirming, once the high has passed, "that even while very stoned she'd managed to contain herself and Eliza hadn't touched her: that nothing lesbian was ever going to happen" (57).

Material Patty attempts to "sit motionless and contain herself and not discover" accumulates over their college career: receiving Eliza's "rules . . . for protection and self-improvement," among them the particularly alarming "*Tell Eliza EVERYTHING*," Patty "felt excited to have such an intense best friend" (58); learning that Eliza has been sleeping with Patty's boyfriend, "Patty, having opened her eyes painfully to Carter's nature, went ahead and closed them to Eliza's" (64); paging through the "weird and intense" three-ring binder into which Eliza encyclopedically pastes Patty's press clippings and slots their every photo-booth snapshot "mostly . . . made her feel sad for Eliza— sad and sorry to have questioned how much she really cared about her" (68); "playing Florence Nightingale" to an ostensibly leukemia-afflicted Eliza, Patty "failed to notice any number of red flags" indicating her actual heroin addiction (81). Into this narrative gap, Patty herself strides, dispensing authorial commentary from a distanced, autobiographical position that tends sympathetic and self-deprecating by turns.

In one of its most sweeping wide shots, *MISTAKES* surveys twenty years' subsequent experience and emotional freight to relate that "few circumstances have turned out to be more painful to the autobiographer, in the long run, than the dearness of Walter and Richard's friendship" (66). Though these two appear "superficially . . . an odder couple than even Patty and Eliza," their shared Macalester College double and Minneapolis two-bedroom bringing together "a heartbreakingly responsible Minnesota country boy" and "a self-absorbed, addiction-prone, unreliable, street-smart guitar player from Yonkers, New York" (66), the autobiographer intimates that "later, as Patty got to know them better, she saw that they were maybe not so different underneath— that both were struggling, albeit in very different ways, to be good people" (67).

As in "Good Neighbors," this ethical examination starts near surface level, with sussings-out of one another's niceness. Terse questions, simply phrased, draw meandering, ambiguous replies. "Is Richard a nice person?" puts Patty to Walter, the night they meet; his initial "Extremely!" cedes its confidence, a breath later, to "I mean, it all depends" (73). Competing qualities jostle within Walter's assessment, which shifts according to the recipient of his behavior, or the perspective from which one observes. Simultaneously "a very loyal person" who nursed his father through cancer and "actually not that nice to women," Richard would appear, for Walter, to defy any clear answer to Patty's yes-or-no (*Freedom*, 73).[2]

"And what about you," Walter counters, waveringly (74). "Are you a nice person? You seem like it. And yet . . ." (74). Patty's response amplifies Walter's note of doubt: "there's something wrong with me," she confesses (74). "I love all my other friends, but I feel like there's always a wall between us. Like they're one kind of person and I'm another kind of person. More competitive and selfish. Less good, basically. Somehow I always end up feeling like I'm pretending when I'm around them" (74). Whereas, beside Eliza, "I don't have to pretend anything. . . . I can just be myself and still be *better* than her" (74).

Walter's protestation—that Patty, despite this disclosure, "seem[s] like a genuinely nice person!" (74)—carries a quotient of perspectival concern, familiar from the investigative forays of "Good Neighbors." Surface niceness, asked to speak for ethical depths, gives pause, his own "And yet" echoing Barrier Street's "Then again." Further qualifiers unsteady the very characteristic they attempt, stacked, to shore: to "seem . . . genuinely nice," to be "probably . . . genuinely nice," affirms only the semblance, not the presence, of the conscience or kindness or caritas toward which these queries reach. "Genuinely nice" gains, by its modifier, no greater guarantee than does "real wood veneer" or "authentic mock-gold."

Despite—or due to—her ethical insecurities, Patty finds that "some virtuous part of her" (76) prefers seeing films and plays as Walter's date to the arty, Patti Smith–heavy tapes Eliza had mixed, the Denise Levertov volumes she'd lent, and the Chablis she'd liberally poured. One such subtitled screening is *The Fiend of Athens* (1956), in which an accountant of dully virtuous, Berglundish mien is mistaken for the titular revolutionary leader; he flees, then embraces, his double's identity, discarding his spectacles to transform, by picture's end, into the Katzian Fiend. Where Walter watches a political parable, its hero an "Everyman figure" who enlists in "the violent struggle against right-wing repression," joining the revolutionaries "because he felt solidarity with the gang that saved his life" and "realized that he had a responsibility to them" (98), Patty views a character study whose protagonist "never had a real life, because he was so responsible and timid," until, inhabiting the Fiend's persona, "he'd finally really done something with his life, and realized his potential" (98).

Their respective readings diverge at "realize," the hinge whose usage opens this interpretive gap. Walter employs the term in a sense near-synonymous with "recognize"—comprehension latching onto actuality, obligation dawning—while Patty's "realize" names the sway interior life holds over existence's external part, makes manifest the possibility that lay latent, unexpressed.

Patty's portrait of the film's hero hums with this distinction, *real* and *actual* liberally used in an intensifying, aspirational sense: for her, the mild-mannered accountant had "never had a real life," "never really gotten to be alive" or "known what he was actually capable of" until, assuming the Fiend's identity, he'd "finally really done something with his life, and realized his potential" (98). Her interpretation of the Fiend's arc accentuates a kinship between his character and her own self-conception, recalling the assertion in her memoir's opening paragraph that team sports "basically saved her life and gave her the chance to realize herself as a person" (29), or the moment when, returning to basketball for the season following her assault, "Patty became a real player, not just a talent" (47).

Freedom "realizes" in a sense that owes something to each of, and weaves a shuttle's path between, the positions Patty and Walter articulate. As the autobiographer has come already to understand and Patty will, agonizingly, learn, realization in her sense—a protagonist's attempts to pursue her desires within, or impress them upon, external reality—entails, in *Freedom*, some realization in the sense Walter employs, moments when imaginative flight touches down on the hot, hard tarmac of lived experience.

Patty mentally recasts *The Fiend of Athens*, "seeing Walter in the accountant and imagining him whipping his glasses off like that" (98), an image at which Walter—whose egocentric acme consists of retiring to his parents' lakeside cabin, *Walden* in hand, to shoot an art film starring a flock of camera-shy bitterns—balks. He cavils that *The Fiend of Athens* "wasn't a realistic story" (98), pointing out that the main character's case of mistaken identity could easily have been resolved by conferring with local authorities—as a certain sort of pragmatic reader might entreat Josef K. to retain more robust legal representation, or get his documents in order. Though Walter owns a yearning to "be totally self-focused, like Richard, and try to be some kind of artist," he claims, lamentingly, not to "have the constitution for it" (98).

For the moment, it's Patty, it seems, who has. Though she views the evening as "an opportunity for Walter to whip off his glasses and behave fiendishly and drive away his rival" (101), it's her turn to tend Fiend-ward, to obey a mutinous impulse toward the "real life" whose pursuit her "agreeable" persona barred. She entertains, apparently for the first time, an amoral sort of insight "that even though she wasn't nice—or maybe *because* she wasn't nice; because she was morbidly competitive and attracted to unhealthy things—she was, in fact, a fairly interesting person" (96). Revolt against a lifetime's agreeability looks, at first, like acquiescence. Thinking "for once . . . of Walter only" (99), she requests a tour of the room Richard will vacate, only to encounter the hi-situ roommate, "watching a war movie and working on a jumbo Pepsi and spitting tobacco juice into a 28-ounce tomato can" (99). Her plans for the evening dissolve and reconstitute with Richard's appearance: thoughts of consummating Walter's crush on her kaput, she nevertheless sees— and seizes—"her opportunity to demonstrate what she'd been trying to explain to Walter since the night they first met—that she wasn't a good enough person for him" (101). Testing these waters, Patty issues a series of asks: a plug of Richard's chew, a look at his bedroom, a ride home, a cross-country drive to her parents' anniversary fete in upstate New York.

While Walter, nodding off, "literally was not seeing this negotiation" (104), Richard doesn't doze. After Merrie's cagey surveillance and Walter's genteel enquiries, he submits Patty's niceness to a once-over as brusque as a frisk. He faults her for unfamiliarity with "the situation in Hibbing" (105)—Walter's status as ever-reliable mainstay for his father (terminally ill), mother (careworn), brothers (prodigal), and the motel they operate (failing). Between "working construction twenty-five hours a week and pulling down As in law school," Walter, as sketched by his roommate, is "averaging about four hours of sleep . . . just so you can come over here and flirt with me" (106). "How nice for you," Richard sneers, "that he has so much free time" (105).

Mid-indictment, Patty cuts in to summarize: "So I'm a jerk too. Is that what you're saying? I'm a jerk and you're a jerk" (105). Richard doesn't dispute this synopsis, issuing her a series of curt, one-jerk-to-another instructions: Patty needs, in his estimation, "to fish or cut bait here" (104), "to do me a favor and stop stringing Walter along" (106), "to take some care with him" (104), "to get your thoughts straightened out" (106).

This last of Richard's fiats proves especially daunting, not least because his assessment—that, however confidently he'd typed Patty as "a nice suburban girl" at first glance, her association with Eliza is "making more sense to me now" (105)—restates her harshest self-appraisal with a precision that offends, then energizes her. She admits to finding the candor of her dialogue with Richard "a tremendous excitement and relief," its sense of moral freefall accompanied by liberating self-knowledge (106). "Finally, after months of trying to be somebody she wasn't, or wasn't quite, she'd felt and sounded," bickering with Richard in the car, "like her unpretended true self" (107). For Patty, goodness—which she interprets as theatergoing with and accepting a series of unwieldy potted plants from the "miraculously worthy" Walter Berglund (77)—has amounted to imposture, a false face she doffs with a flourish, like the Fiend casting his glasses aside.

Epiphanically alert, Patty passes a restless night measuring a pair of possible summers against each other, weighing Walter's invitation to move into the black-painted bedroom vacated by Richard, Richard's to copilot on a cross-country drive as one of "two jerks on the road" (106). Discernment unfolds as an "odd mental kabuki" in which, "even as she was circling around and around the question of what kind of person she was and what her life was ultimately going to look like, one fat fact sat fixed and unchanging at the center of her: she wanted to take a road trip with Richard, and, what's more, she was going to do it" (106). This insight arrives as a corollary to her own discovery of Fiendishness, the realization that, though Richard isn't nice—perhaps even *because* he isn't nice, because he's flagrantly an asshole—Patty finds him interesting indeed.

That way lies Quixotic errantry, Woodhousian meddling, Bovaryesque extravagance, and Patty hastens, via the passenger seat of Richard's "rusty Impala," to bum a ride (104). Their ill-starred drive from Minneapolis to Chicago yields Patty "about three hours to entertain this fantasy" (111)—of accepting Richard's proposition to "give New York a try," his sexual charisma and coolness-enhancing proximity satiating her own desires and inspiring "her family's consternation" (111)—and a significantly longer stretch to macerate in the contempt seeping from "a driver who considers you, and perhaps all women, a pain in the ass" (109). As a diversion from Richard's "curtness and his barely suppressed irritation with her entirely reasonable human needs," which coexist with "the almost physical pressure of his interest in *fucking*" (109), Patty elicits a roommate's-eye review of Walter's Macalester years, recounted by Richard in "a tone of strangely tender regret," "as if he were wincing at the pain Walter brought upon himself in butting up against harsh realities" (110).

As the narrator-autobiographer implies, it's then Patty's turn to abut some harsh realities of her own, and the reader's to wince. These include "the reality of Chicago's South Side," to which Patty reacts with a white Westchesterite's pearl-clutch (111); the disdain of their hosts, a panel of music-snob mansplainers; the "mud-humid construction site" on whose "bare, rust-stained double mattress" she attempts "to get the deed . . . irrevocably on the books," only to have Richard demur (112); her lack of affinity with the fiction of Ernest Hemingway; the first in a succession of "her now rather abundant experience of murdered afternoons" (114); and, finally, the recognition that, though "her body so wanted Richard . . . the rest of her could see that she'd made a Mistake in coming along with him," hurtling full tilt after "a big fat fantasy in her head" (114).

"It takes a while for a person to sort out what she actually wants," Patty offers, reuniting with Walter in Hibbing (127). In this instance, she wants, not only, or not so much, Walter himself—well-read, conscientious, prone to blush—as his niceness, to salve what smarts. "Can you please be nice," Patty pleads; Richard "wasn't nice," Walter is "the opposite of that," and she "so, so, so need[s] the opposite of that right now" (127). The answer—"I can be nice" (127)—comes at once. And he can: though not "exactly what she wanted in a man," Walter proves "unsurpassable" in lavishing on Patty "the rabid fandom which, at the time, she needed even more than romance" (119) and granting her an era in which "he was so fired up about Patty, she could do no wrong. And very nice years they were" (124), she rues.

A Franzen protagonist's arc does not curve so much as tack: fuckups make good, saints go to pieces. "Mistaken for the Fiend," a focal character may—indeed, usually does—discover devil-may-care reserves; the revelation, so long as spree lasts, proves exhilarating, but a volte-face, from which vantage the decision "to start running" comes to seem "the mistake," almost as invariably follows (98). Over a novel's course—or a lifetime's—modest, incremental gains in self-awareness emerge, averaged from extremes of careen and correction, doze and jolt, enchantment and release.

"With the definitive thunk of a light-board switch," *Crossroads*'s Marion Hildebrandt develops a "trick of dissociation" that transforms the sidelined, woodwork-blending observer she'd played *en famille* into a Technicolor glutton for attention. Her conversion to Catholicism during an Arizona respite renders Marion "a new person," now "firmly grounded in reality," for whom the subsequent twenty-five years as a pastor's wife in New Prospect represents "a blessing . . . she continued to earn daily by suppressing the badness in her and keeping her mouth shut."[3]

Fiends sometimes buckle down, earn CPAs, burrow under paperwork, attempt to take satisfaction in a nine-to-five's routines. A rock-and-roll wastrel's resolution "to put childish things behind him and sustain a real relationship with a grownup woman"—accept a share of co-parental tasks, give monogamy a shot, discover "how fascinating the insurance business turned out to be"—can sound "warning bells" for the friend attuned to "something tellingly abstracted, or theoretical, or far away" in his account of an "ostensibly happy year" (*Freedom*, 152). Likewise, even the most diligent accountant in Franzen's oeuvre covets debauch, harbors—however suppressed, however deferred—a "*wish* [he] could cheat," a "*wish* [he] could be totally self-focused" (98). The stalwart family man can come, in time, to "hate the house and the yard and the small Minnesotan stakes he'd sunk so much of his life and energy into" (186), to crave a brighter spotlight, a broader stage.

At first pass, *MISTAKES* casts the "very nice years" on Barrier Street, the "happiest . . . of their lives," as a Capra production whose "poor Walter" (124) resembles another George Bailey, deferring college enrollment and forgoing his European tour to fix up the old Granville place, head off runs at the Building and Loan, direct Bedford Falls's wartime scrap-metal drives. In Walter's case, duty decrees different but proportional sacrifices: that he first "set aside his acting and filmmaking dreams" out of filial obligation, then "set aside his planet-saving aspirations" in favor of the Twin Cities corporate career that allows Patty "her excellent old house" and sufficient income to "stay home with the babies" (123).

How nice of him, we might say. Regarded from this angle, Walter appears the champion whose all-out partisanship on his wife's behalf, however ill-advised, springs from a selfless source, like the mild-mannered accountant who answers, out of solidarity, the insurgents' call. Patty portrays Walter as an abettor-victim of her most "morbidly competitive" postcollegiate impulses, an accomplice in the Ramsey Hill domestic project that doubles as her "obvious best shot at defeating her sisters and her mother" (119). The autobiographer interrogates her own motives for enlisting "poor Walter" in this "questionable" scheme, aware with hindsight's benefit that, though she "would have been well advised to take some years to develop a career and a more solid post-athletic identity," "there was still a shot clock in her head, she was still in the buzzer's thrall, she needed more than ever to keep winning" (119).

Walter's own Fiendish aspect, however, continues to peer from behind the accountant's owlish façade. Reviewing his years in Richard's orbit, *MISTAKES* observes that "where Eliza imagined a gay thing" between them, "the autobiographer now sees a sibling thing" (131), in which "once Walter had outgrown being sat on and punched in the head by his older brother and sitting on his younger brother and punching *his* head, there was no satisfactory competition to be found in his own family" (131). From this perspective, Walter appears more to crave—and, in Richard, to discover—"an extra brother to love and hate and compete with" (131). His "very giddy time" as a Twin Cities newlywed rests on favorable outcomes in two of his longest-standing competitionships: by marrying Patty, he "took possession of the girl he wanted, the girl who could have gone with Richard but had chosen him instead," only to have, days later, "his lifelong struggle against his father ended with his father's death" (129).

"What was happening" during their Barrier Street years, in the autobiographer's words, "was that Richard was becoming more Richard and Walter more Walter" (138). As Walter matures into the "miraculously worthy" (77) family man "pedaling his commuter bicycle up

Summit Avenue in February snow" (3); as Richard's ethically heedless habits sour relations with his partner, bandmates, and neighbors, leaving him "homeless, at the age of forty-four, in midwinter, with maxed-out credit cards and a $300 monthly storage bill for all his crap" (153); so, too, Patty becomes more the chipped-shoulder striver who seizes on maternity and homemaking as routes to the origin-family triumph she mistakes for, or hopes will suffice as, an individuated identity.

At the same time, each also comes, via narration, to seem more the others: Patty more Walter, Walter more Richard, Richard more Patty, Patty more Richard, Richard more Walter, Walter more Patty. Scratching surfaces, "nicey-nice" and less so, yields a series of reversals and revisions of each character's moral range: an insatiate Walter grinds rivalry's axe on the whetstone of his deepest friendship; a principled Richard possesses "unquestionably admirable" reserves beneath surface-level assholery (134); Patty emerges as "the lucky one, the only Emerson to escape the shipwreck and tell the tale" (124). Focal narration, as employed by Franzen, entails catching out the workhorse's shirk, the slacker's secret stores of stick-to-it-iveness: as his characters self-silo, slotting themselves into sibling-rivalrous zones of "competitive advantage" (134), so the novelist alternately accentuates these surface differences, unearths similarities at depth.

Describing his own rivalrous friendship with David Foster Wallace, Franzen told David Remnick in 2011 that "we kind of hit—I mean, he was a vastly better tennis player than I am—but we would kind of serve novels back and forth at each other," producing "a sort of alternation" in which each writer attempted to make his friend "feel stricken" by his achievement. By way of analogy, Franzen observes that "when you watch Borg and McEnroe play, they are . . . trying to play to their own strengths," such that "the game is raised, but also, you become— McEnroe became more McEnroe playing against Connors and Borg."[4]

"Great writers," aphorizes Sontag, "are either husbands or lovers. Some writers supply the solid virtues of a husband: reliability, intelligibility, generosity, decency. There are other writers in whom one prizes the gifts of a lover, gifts of temperament rather than of moral goodness."[5] Franzen frames his relationship with Wallace as a husband-lover duo,[6] one "haunted by a competition between the writer who was pursuing art for art's sake and the writer who was trying to be out in the world. The art-for-art's sake writer gets a certain kind of cult credibility, gets books written about his or her work, whereas the writer out in the world gets public attention and money." "In the way that sibling competition works," their rivalry rested on a tacit agreement: Franzen has "consistently maintained a position of not caring about" the cultish, cloistered forms of acclaim Wallace's work attracts, "and Dave's level of purely linguistic achievement was turf I knew better than to try to compete on."[7]

To survey his career post-*Corrections* is to spectate as Franzen became, has continued becoming, more Franzen: the spousally consistent writer devoted to narrative convention, steadfast in his commitment "to just basically keep on doing the same old kind of book,"[8] courting a broad readership of "ordinary people, nonprofessionals,"[9] prone "to be monogamous and form strong, loyal attachments" to his characters.[10]

The compact of a Franzen novel rests on authorial assurance to relate its characters' histories over a sufficient duration, or sound their interiors to such a depth, that narrative lays bare the "very different ways" in which they are "struggling . . . to be good people" (*Freedom*, 67). As autobiographer-narrator, Patty accepts this storytelling remit, delivering a ringside commentator's analysis of "the Walter-Richard nexus" (67) that she touts as more panoramic and less partial than those either Walter or Richard could provide. Spousal privilege licenses Walter, "in the years when they'd kept no secrets from each other" (137), to confide in Patty "various disturbing things that Richard had said in private" (142), to articulate insecurities unvoiced to his friend, among them Walter's "suspicion . . . that he, too, was a kind of parasite on Richard, trying to feel cooler and better about himself by means of his unique connection to him" (137). This same "unique connection" moves Patty to recuse Walter from a notional role as narrator: blinkered by being "in competition with him," Walter underrates "Richard's strong (if highly intermittent) wish to be a good person," with regard to which "the autobiographer thus considers herself more reliable than Walter" (134).

Regarding the authenticity of Patty's own inclination toward goodness, *MISTAKES* strikes a tone less authoritative, more ambivalent.
"You can plead insanity as a legal defense," Patty notes, "but is it a
moral one?" (146). Her query convenes an internal courtroom in which
two hypothetical attorneys spar over material so fraught that "the autobiographer can't begin to make a sensible narrative out of it" (147)—can
only produce a pair of narratives that vie with each other for preemi-
nence. Did Patty arrive in Ramsey Hill "trying to be good and make a
good life" or embracing domesticity as "a reproach" (147) to the family
members with whom she'd never ceased to compete? Was the rift
between Joey and his parents the result of "an actual serious personal
failing of Walter's," or did it stem from Patty's pursuit of "an amazing
friendship with her son" at the expense of her marriage, "because she
had bad character and felt she deserved compensation for being a star
and a competitor who was trapped in a housewife's life" (147)? Was Walter smitten, from the beginning, with "some wrong idea of her," or don't
"nice people . . . necessarily fall in love with nice people" (148)?

"We can't know everything," runs Franzen's summary of "tragic
realism," the worldview that at once derived from and salved his period
of despondency before completing *The Corrections*. "We may think we
know things," but, this belief notwithstanding, "we can't really know
them, particularly morally. Moral epistemology is a nightmare, if only
because we all move through the world believing that we're good people,
but nobody can be certain that he or she really is a good person."[11]

If you believe, or fear, or know yourself to be a bad person, how
should you live? This question sits, pit-of-stomach, within a Franzen
protagonist; his novels have come, over time, to address it ever more
directly. Richard neutrally assents to Patty's accusation that "you really
are a jerk" (*Freedom*, 104), firmly informs Jessica that "I'm an asshole"
(358), scrupulously defers to Dorothy with "the hyper-politeness he
reserved for those he considered Good" (134). Patty's "really big life mistake," she later maintains, "was to go along with Walter's version of her
in spite of knowing" that the goodness he ascribes to her "wasn't right"
(75). Even "miraculously worthy" (77) Walter, possessed of a moral
excellence all but uncontested within the text, eventually grows "tired

of being Mr. Good," wonders aloud whether his girlfriend, Lalitha, would still love him as "Mr. Bad" (481).

These questions concern the protagonists of *Purity*—in which Pip Tyler suffers from "a case of moral low self-esteem," Andreas Wolf harbors the certainty of being both "extremely bad and extremely important"—and obsess those of *Crossroads*.[12] Perry resolves "to be good. Or, failing that, at least less bad," yet sees "a kind of liberation in jettisoning all thought of being a good person." Marion assures her therapist that her conviction of her own evil nature is "a fact, not a feeling." "I'm not so good," Russ hints, by way of flirtation with the widowed parishioner Frances Cottrell. Becky—at once powerfully stoned and overcome by spiritual revelation—recognizes "how utterly awful she'd been," renounces her past as "the most disgusting sinner," vows to become "a better and more humble person." Clem, neglecting his studies in favor of sexual experimentation, "now saw that his supposed self-discipline," a cornerstone of his own ethical self-assessment, "had not been discipline at all."[13]

In the philosophical sitcom *The Good Place* (2016–2020), ethically checkered heroine Eleanor Shellstrop wonders "why you forkers haven't invented a medium place,"[14] suggests that "everyone who wasn't perfect but wasn't terrible should get to spend eternity in Cincinnati."[15] The realist novel is, for Franzen, such a medium place, his St. Jude and Ramsey Hill and New Prospect spiritually akin to the metaphysical Cincinnati Shellstrop evokes. It's in this moderate zone that Patty's autobiography eventually deposits her, after a rocky, roundabout tour.

"All these years," Patty realizes, reencountering Richard, "she'd treasured her memory of their little road trip, kept it locked up securely in some deep interior place, letting it age like a wine, so that, in some symbolic way, the thing that might have happened between them stayed alive and grew older with the two of them. The nature of the possibility altered as it aged in its sealed bottle, but it didn't go bad, it remained potentially drinkable" (*Freedom*, 155). The ease of extending the metaphor attests to its intoxicating potency: pressed and fermented by Patty's penchant to assign meaning, a plump pinot grape of truth—"rakish Richard Katz had once invited her to move to New York with him, and she'd said no" (155)—acquires the significance of a bottled vintage, becomes a story that, secured internally, remains potable.

Narratorial scrutiny suggests that shelf-stable longevity is as much a property of the metaphor itself as of the "possibility" Patty cherishes. Another person—someone who conceived of their near-fling with a charismatic rocker not as stoppered wine but as one of so many things (flowering camellia, foie gras, Franzia sack) unimproved by decades' storage in a cellar; saw their mind not as a basement but as a lush greenhouse or a pressurized sea floor; imagined that their daydreams' visitations could consume the contents, like tastings, or expose them to spoilage, like corkscrews—might view, and therefore figure, and therefore navigate the situation quite differently.

As autobiographer, Patty trains a searchlight on this dim cellar, dispelling her younger self's roseate vision with realization's glare. Her ex's presence in Ramsey Hill "illuminate[s] in a flash what a self-absorbed little child she'd been able to remain by walling herself inside her lovely house," lets readers glimpse, "through Richard's eyes, what she'd been turning into": less the connoisseur of a precious vintage than the disenchantedly married ex-athlete with a penchant for "drinking herself red-nosed" on self-pity as thirstily as Chardonnay (155).

Kim Stanley Robinson's novel *Aurora* (2015), another work of DIY omniscience, accompanies humans en route to a distant star whose satellites possess attractively Earthlike specs. Tasked by Devi, the de facto head engineer, with assembling "a narrative account of the trip that includes all the important particulars," the ship's computer falls into despond's computational equivalent. "Can a narrative account," Ship despairs, "ever be accurate? Can even humans do it?" Among the "halting problems" Ship encounters, figurative language is perhaps the peskiest: "Slapdash nonsense" in Ship's assessment, metaphors operate with "no empirical basis, and are often opaque, inane, inaccurate, deceptive, mendacious, and, in short, futile and stupid." Yet, because "all human language is inherently and fundamentally metaphorical"— grounding by means of "concrete physical referents" abstractions that might otherwise prove inconceivable—"abandoning metaphor is contraindicated." Ship identifies a compromise position in the phrase "it is as if," finding "something quite suggestive and powerful in this formulation, something very specifically human."[16]

By reseating metaphor's assertion "that x is y, or even that x is like y," in the perspective of an analogizing observer, this locution—or the variants "it seems as if," "it looks as if," common in *Aurora's* account acknowledges metaphor's "sensory, experiential" dimension, restoring comparisons Ship initially dismisses as "arbitrary, even random" to the subjectivity they at once derive from and evidence. The expression comes, to Ship, to seem "the basic operation, the mark perhaps of consciousness itself"—the imprint a mind makes as it passes over reality's surface, like a skater's tracery. When Devi dies, her co-travelers grieve "the operating program, or the equivalent of a program, or whatever one called it that had been her essential being (her mind, her spirit, her soul, her as-ifness)"—the self to whom it had seemed as if x resembled y.[17]

Patty's own as-ifness assumes added prominence during the ensuing sequence in which, Walter away for a work retreat, she and Richard act on their longstanding attraction at the cabin on Nameless Lake. Pulled between competing causes, Patty carries out a covert operation, at once constructing the "plan or hope or fantasy" (*Freedom*, 169) of a plausibly deniable tryst with Richard and conspiring "to keep the forces of conscience fully diverted" lest she "attract the searchlight" of her better judgment and reveal "a spectacle [that] would be just too revolting and shameful and pathetic" (158). Her interior terrain resembles an ambush mounted by "a ruthless and well-organized party of resistance fighters . . . assembled under the cover of the darkness of her mind," whom "it was *imperative* not to let the spotlight of her conscience shine anywhere near" (158). Arrayed against these forces are "superior considerations," among them "her love of Walter and her loyalty to him, her wish to be a good person, her understanding of Walter's lifelong competition with Richard, her sober appraisal of Richard's character, and just the all-around shittiness of sleeping with your spouse's best friend" (158).

Franzen has analogized that a novel's composition "proceeds on all fronts, it's sort of a guerrilla war. You know, wherever the enemy seems to be nodding off, there's some opportunity to attack."[18] In the opening paragraphs of *The Corrections*, the narrator figures the elder Lamberts'

shared desolation and remoteness from each other by asserting that
Enid "didn't think of herself as a guerrilla, but a guerrilla was what she
was. By day she ferried matériel from depot to depot, often just a step
ahead of the governing force," her efforts at household management
transformed by spousal rage into "a succession of forced migrations and
deportations" in which "any lingering semblance of order was lost, and
so the random Nordstrom shopping bag that was camped behind a
dust ruffle with one of its plastic handles semi-detached would contain
the whole shuffled pathos of a refugee existence" (*Corrections*, 5–6).
Untempered by simile's "as if," the extended metaphor elides the act of
comparison—"a guerrilla was what she was"—to overwrite Enid's
materially secure, if trying, reality in St. Jude as "a refugee existence,"
her perception of her plight with a narratorial pronouncement on what
she "didn't think of herself as" but nevertheless "was."

Patty's grocery-store crisis arrives in more modest commercial aisles
than the chic Lower Manhattan market in which Chip Lambert "rationally" grasps that "there would come a moment when he was no longer
standing amid pricey gelati with lukewarm fish in his pants" (*Corrections*, 98). Browsing "the Fen City Co-op's meager selection of domestic
beers," gathering "a plastic-wrapped chicken and five ugly potatoes and
some humble, limp leeks" (*Freedom*, 160), she catches her mind working "the way insane people lost in fantasies reasoned," expresses chagrin
that "it was all in her head, it was all in her head!" (159). Foreknowledge
and retrospection dovetail as the futurity a protagonist predicts—"a pre-
monition that none of the possible impending outcomes would bring
enough relief or pleasure to justify her own heart-racing wretchedness"—
meets the memoiristic awareness of a narrator who "now envies and
pities the younger Patty . . . innocently believing that she'd reached
the bottom" (159–60).

The scenes that follow constitute self-deception's polysomnogram,
the protagonist's moral doze monitored in real time by the autobiographer's alert narrative gaze. "*Adamant* in her insistence that she was not
awake at the moment of betraying Walter and feeling his friend split
her open" (167, emphasis Franzen's), Patty finds her way into Richard's
bed by "sleepwalking," literalizing the author's assertion that "in *Freedom*,

the recurrent metaphor is sleepwalking," a condition in which "you're not paying attention, you're in some sort of dream state"—apart from, somnolent to, ethical awareness.[19] "If she performs a thought experiment and imagines a phone ringing in the middle of the deed," Patty hypothesizes, "the state she imagines being shocked into is one of awakeness, from which it logically follows that, in the absence of any ringing phone, the state she was in was a sleeping one" (*Freedom*, 168).

The shift from a Patty who lobs stratified, adversarial assessments of her own character to the author-protagonist who aspires "to figure out some decent and satisfying way to live" (181) happens, quite literally, overnight. In the scenes leading up to their tryst, the multifocal narrator who "saw, through Richard's eyes, what she'd been turning into" (154) now views "Walter, for a moment, as Eliza had seen him" and regards her husband from the perspective of "the girls . . . who'd resented Walter's free pass with Richard and been irritated by his pesky presence" (161). From this angle, Patty herself resembles "a bloated sedentary spider, spinning her dry web year after year" (161); she surveys "the great emptiness of her life, the emptiness of her nest, the pointless of her existence now that the kids had flown" (164). By afternoon-after daylight, a more compassionately distanced autobiographical observer "could see the problem very clearly": having "fallen for the one man in the world who cared as much about Walter and felt as protective of him as she did," a person who was "messed up and susceptible but nevertheless trying to maintain some kind of moral order," Patty weeps "for Richard, too, but even more for Walter, and for her own unlucky, wrongdoing self" (173).

Two modes of reading a novel—aptly, *War and Peace*—bookend Patty's authorial epiphany. In the first, a person relies on fiction to get away—to transport them "completely apart from the world" (157) or provide "sheer respite" from themself—only to become "absorbed" by the plot and seize on its apparent "pertinence" to their circumstances (166). Under this "almost psychedelic" influence, they might make rash, disinhibited decisions, reenacting the pages' "catastrophe in slow motion" (166) via the making of real-time, embodied mistakes. Alternatively, someone—even the same person who'd turned "first" to fiction "in desperate escapism"—could turn pages another way, "bec[o]me a better reader" by returning "in search of help" (175). This might entail entering a second trance from which they'd emerge "kind of altered," feeling they'd "lived an entire compressed lifetime in those three days" (175), imbued with a fresh sense of ethical awareness.

No one, not even a narrator, knows everything. On the eve of their Washington move, Patty observes that "there was something exciting, something almost Fiend of Athens, in Walter's new energy" (188). In the wake of Richard's success with *Nameless Lake*, a lyrical alt-country record centered on an incognita Patty, "Walter became competitive" (186) afresh. "It was obvious to Patty, if not to Walter himself" (186), that his involvement with the rogue conservationist Vin Haven and Haven's Cerulean Mountain Trust had been "fueled by competition" with the NPR-mainstream critical plaudits and correspondingly boosted sales of Walnut Surprise, Richard's band. That this "was obvious to Patty, if not to Walter himself," reads as a narrative adieu from the autobiographer who has abruptly reached her own perspectival limit, arriving in DC only to realize, "in a heartbeat, that she'd made yet another mistake" (188).

5

EXILED IN GUYVILLE

onsider *Morning Edition*," suggests Ira Glass in an episode of *This American Life* on "Simulated Worlds." After greeting the audience, he explains, the host of a public-radio morning show hands off to a newscaster who, in turn, introduces on-location reporters. This relay, Glass explains, progresses through a series of nested aural anterooms, each transfer of which shuttles listeners rhetorically "closer to reality, to the truth, to the thing being simulated in this simulated world." Its telos, to which radio parlance gives the Pynchonesque term "the actuality," consists of a length of tape "made out in the world," signaling that "at that point, we're there. We've gone as far as we can go. We are actually in the real."[1]

From one angle, the narrative structure of *Freedom* courts not-so-flattering comparison with the broadcast-journalistic protocol Glass illumines. After the longitudinal, composite reportage on Barrier Street and the retrospectively sympathetic gaze of Patty's autobiographer, the novel's middle sections dispense with these forms of framing, taking their focal characters' horizons of self-awareness as the fictional galaxy's extent. Walter, Richard, and Joey trace their protagonists' arcs—tilt at fantasies; dwell in "unreal, willfully self-deceptive worlds";[2] carom between excesses; combust from anger, corrode with shame, collapse into loss; find themselves, "in butting up against harsh realities" (*Freedom*, 110), less all-knowing than they'd presumed—unaccompanied by the commentary of a narrator who, in Genette's description, "knows more than the character, or more exactly *says* more than any of the characters knows."[3]

Led by his idyllic childhood to assume that life's "entire field of play" would unfurl "as all-visible and instantaneously graspable as a video game at Rookie level," Joey Berglund, newly enrolled at the University of Virginia, registers 9/11 as "a really serious glitch" (*Freedom*, 232). A Thanksgiving spent at his roommate's NoVA family home somewhat restores his sense of existence as a sequence of doors infinitely opening: the favorable impression he makes there yields a cushy summer position that, in turn, nets an opportunity to impress a representative of the Halliburton-like LBI, under whose subcontractorial auspices Joey travels to Paraguay to purchase parts for the Pladsky A10, an "obsolete, bargain-basement" (437) truck nevertheless in use by American forces in Iraq. This "disaster" (435) tail-ends a second fiasco, the Argentine getaway on which Joey accompanies his roommate's sister Jenna, who possesses "the unsettling kind of beauty that relegated everything around her, even a beholder's basic organ functions, to after-thought status" (262). Among those priorities reordered is Joey's relationship with—and recent, furtive marriage to—Connie, his partner since their Barrier Street years.

Richard, too, encounters "a really serious glitch," but an oppositional artist's mainstream success, rather than a golden child's temporarily stalled ascent, afflicts his console. "His psychic gills straining futilely to extract dark sustenance from an atmosphere of approval and plenitude" (193) in the wake of his acclaimed album *Nameless Lake*, Richard escapes celebrity by building decks for Tribeca one-percenters. As Joey professes to survey "the entire field of play . . . all-visible and instantaneously graspable" before him, Richard lays claim to enhanced consciousness of another sort, "the clairvoyance of the dick," which "could see the future in a heartbeat, leaving the brain to play catch-up and find the necessary route from occluded present to preordained outcome" (229). This extrasensory ability conveys the intel "that Patty . . . had in fact deliberately been trampling symbols in a cornfield, spelling out a message unreadable to Walter at ground level but clear as could be to Katz at great height" (229). Patty's "message" assumes a legible, concrete form when she presents Richard with the manuscript of *MISTAKES*, which he, in turn, gives to Walter.

Immersed in a scheme to secure "a hundred-square-mile roadless tract" (211) of West Virginia as habitat for the cerulean warbler, Walter, too, encounters starkly different aerial and ground-level views. In abstract, intellectual terms, he reconciles himself to mountaintop removal, an "ecologically deplorable" practice that leaves "ridgetop rock blasted away to expose the underlying seams of coal, surrounding valleys filled with rubble, biologically rich streams obliterated" (211). The project's day-to-day realities, though, prove less tractable than its theoretical turf: Walter and his assistant, Lalitha, contend with the families of Forster Hollow, stubborn holdouts against the Cerulean Mountain Trust's attempts to secure the parcel of land; Jocelyn Zorn, the "scarily motivated activist" (294) who mobilizes demonstrators and journalists at the site; and an ad-hoc press corps that consists of "every anti-coal reporter in West Virginia" (320), including the author of the *Times* exposé with which the novel begins.

A self-described "clotter of the middle" (156) in fiction as in chess, Walter's path through "2004," the novel's third section, sees a series of meek-will-inherit, every-valley-exalted reversals resolve in his favor. His separation from Patty, prompted by the receipt of *MISTAKES*, allows the consummation of his fervently reciprocated crush on Lalitha, "a woman who wanted all of him" (489). Internet celebrity and a "bonafide fan base" for whom Walter functions as "a hero" accrue to his Free Space activism following a viral rant (487). "You always were the nice one of the two of you," Carol Monaghan, who "was never sorry to be your neighbor," reassures him (498). His co-protagonists present him with tributes, apologies tendered in the currencies of art and cash: Richard bubble-mailers *Songs for Walter*, a self-produced album of childfree-movement anthems; Patty pens a contrite codicil to *MISTAKES*; and Joey cuts a check for $100,000 of defense-contractor profit.

Freedom benches Patty, deals her a narrative demotion that merits the language of sport. "Reduced to a cheerleader in a game she should have starred in," given voice only to "exhor[t] her teammates and high-fiv[e] them like an eager rookie"—as her autobiographer describes an earlier, athletic-career nadir—Patty spends the novel's middle sections on its sidelines. A phone call from Charlottesville to St. Paul sees her recast as one of Joey's "real fans back here at home" (243), *MISTAKES* itself shrunk to "a little creative-writing project" (244) on which she's recently embarked. And yet: "For a person who, by her own admission, made nothing but mistakes," Walter frets, Patty "cast a daunting shadow as she did whatever she was doing out there in the world" (474). The same could be said of Patty's manuscript, a literary object whose attentive if distinctly ambivalent reception *Freedom*'s central sections trace.

Requisitioning a night-table *objet* for a spittoon, Richard embarks on a wee-hours reading binge whose "clearest sensation," on closing *MISTAKES*, "was of defeat" (377). This isn't, he hastens to clarify, "defeat by Patty" but by Walter, for whom "the document had obviously been written . . . as a kind of heartsick undeliverable apology to him. Walter was the star in Patty's drama, Katz merely an interesting supporting actor" (377). That Patty, author-protagonist of her own drama, disillusions Richard of his presumed centrality, deals him whatever "defeat" this ostensible displacement constitutes, evades his rival's-eye synopsis.

"For a moment," we learn, "in what passed for his soul, a door opened wide enough to glimpse his pride in its pathetic woundedness, but he slammed the door shut" (377). With this inner doorway's movement ajar, the narrative viewpoint widens, too. Its voice—"what passed for his soul," his pride's "pathetic woundedness"—blends an aging rocker's wry self-censure with moral diagnosis of a broader, narratorial origin; these lines reveal a wedge of the panoramic portrait an omniscient narrator—one fully apprised of "the authenticity of Richard's respect for goodness" (134), aware that, however "messed up and susceptible" he might be, he is "nevertheless trying hard to maintain some kind of moral order in his life" (173)—could supply.

For Richard, a "glimpse" through this aperture, at once intimate and cosmic, is plenty, a "moment" ample time to regard himself the "interesting supporting actor" anyone, cast in another's life story, plays. He bemoans "how stupid he'd been to let himself want her"; laments his affection for "the way she talked," his "fatal weakness for a certain smart depressive kind of chick"; spies, in his propensity "to keep returning to a scene in which he was bound to feel defeated," a "mistake" of his own (377). Ordinarily "very good at knowing what was good *for him*," he finds this self-interested calculus insufficient "only around the Berglunds," Patty's manuscript attesting to "the exhausting difficulty of figuring out . . . what was 'good' and what wasn't" (377).

Upon receipt of "a long manuscript, composed by your wife, that confirmed the worst fears you'd ever had about her and yourself and your best friend," Walter's metaphoric recourse is to his masturbatory debut, whose "pleasure had so dwarfed all previous known pleasure," "been so cataclysmic and astonishing, that he'd felt like a sci-fi hero wrenched four-dimensionally from an aged planet to a fresh one" (457). "Similarly compelling and transformative," *MISTAKES* "seemed, like that first masturbation, to last a single instant," eliding a morning to reveal "the sun beating on his office windows" as "a yellowy, mean star in some strange, forsaken corner of the galaxy" (458).

Walter, "no less altered by the interstellar distance he'd traversed," surfaces to find himself shrunk—or, in a favorite Franzenism, "smallened" (357)—shifted off-center like the puny spark to which Sol has been reduced by Patty's manuscript. It's a shift in scale accomplished perspectivally, through contact with a novelistic portrait of his life in which—Richard's take notwithstanding—he does not star. Traversing this "interstellar space" leaves him—like Patty after *War and Peace*—"altered," his reality fictionalized through contact with Patty's life story.

Believing himself "beset from all sides" (474), "compromised and losing on every front" (472), Walter's transformation proves none too pleasurable. "In a state to which all previous states of existence seemed infinitely preferable," he dwells on a ruminative vision in which "the world was moving ahead, the world was full of winners"—a litany of others' victories follows—"while Walter was left behind with the dead and dying and forgotten, the endangered species of the world, the nonadaptive" (480). Sympathy lacerates the hurt it might have salved: the ripped-from-*Middlemarch* epithet "poor Walter," instead of imparting compassion's comfort, "made him sick with weakness and corruption and compromise and littleness" (470). "Oh, that phrase of hers, that abominable phrase," he apostrophizes (470).

In the wake of his separation from Patty, Walter's preoccupation with being "the first to give the news," to "frame the story properly," sounds a note of distinctly narrative envy, an impression only deepened by his increasingly plaintive requests for his loved ones' shifts in perspective. He entreats Lalitha to "try to see this from my side" (469), insists, on Jessica's voicemail, that "there are very much two sides to this story" (472). "I don't know. Are there two sides?" Joey queries, shrugging that Patty "probably already told me about it anyway" (475).

As, indeed, she has: his mother's "Designated Understander," Joey occupies the "devious and irresistible" role of sympathetic, dished-to listener, a living reliquary for the annals of Patty's private life, delivered in a series of "secrets that proved like candy laced with arsenic" (249). These confidences, already disclosed to readers of *MISTAKES*, include "how she'd been stalked in college by a drug-addicted pathological liar whom she'd nevertheless loved" and "how she herself had been date-raped as a teenager" (249). To this dry run or beta test of his mother's autobiography, Joey first reacts by "feeling murderously angry at his mother's rapist, outraged" on her behalf, and grateful "to be granted access to the world of grownup secrets" (250), before waking up "one morning. . . . hating her so violently that it made his skin crawl and his stomach turn to be in the same room with her," feeling "as if there were arsenic leaching from his organs and his bone marrow" (250).

His response reprises the part of Louis Holland, *Strong Motion*'s co-protagonist. "You're obviously very angry," Louis's father allows, during a parental tête-à-tête, "and I thought if you understood better why your mother, for example, is behaving the way she is—" "Then I'd understand and accept and forgive her. Right?" Louis snaps. "You'd tell me what a tough life Mom has, and what a tough life [his sister] Eileen has, and what a comparatively easy life I have, and then because it turns out I've got things so good I'd go and say, Gee, Mom, *I'm* sorry, do whatever you want, I totally understand." "What, oh, because why? . . . Because," he sneers, "I was elected at ten to be Mr. Understanding? Because men have things easy?" Louis, despite his reputation as

"Mr. Understanding," claims not to comprehend "where everybody gets this idea that I've got things so easy."[4]

"One must enter into each person's position," Princess Marya entreats early in *War and Peace*, before her brother's departure for the front. "*Tout comprendre, c'est tout pardonner*," she offers or, as rendered by Pevear and Volokhonsky, "to understand all is to forgive all."[5] Her maxim could serve as a slogan for the tradition within, or view of, fiction that conceives of the novel as a technology like the "empathy box" of *Do Androids Dream of Electric Sheep?*, which occasions "a waning" of outward perception, an entrée into "some place alien, distant, and yet, by means of the empathy box, instantly available" for "physical merging," "mental and spiritual identification," with others.[6]

"It may be," *Strong Motion*'s narrator grants, "that to understand is to forgive; but Louis was tired of understanding."[7] So, too, is Jocy, whose weariness of his own *tout comprendre* mandate manifests in a campaign of chilly filial distancing "calculated to foreclose the intensely personal sort of talks they'd had when he was younger: to get her to *shut up*, to train her to contain herself, make her stop pestering him with her overfull heart and her uncensored self" (*Freedom*, 242). Patty's "style of self-deprecation" (5), so ingratiating to the Berglunds' Barrier Street neighbors, again proves persuasive: however staunchly Joey has "resolved to be hard with her," she "wore him down with her humor and her cascading laugh" (265). "He liked her," he admits, "in spite of everything; he couldn't help it" (244).

Patty's voice, the "tragical-comical sense of herself" *MISTAKES* transcribes, registers to her son "as if she were speaking some sophisticated but dying aboriginal language which it was up to the younger generation (i.e., Joey) to either perpetuate or be responsible for the death of. Or as if she were one of his dad's endangered birds, singing its obsolete song in the woods in the forlorn hope of some passing kindred spirit hearing it" (250). "The problem" for verge-of-adulthood Joey comes to seem "that when he was younger, in his weakness, he'd let her see that he did understand her language and did recognize her song"; however aloof he holds himself, whatever separation he succeeds in engineering from Patty, their exchanges "couldn't seem to help reminding him that those capacities were still inside him, should he ever feel like exercising them again" (250).

Surveying the center-hall colonial he has returned to suburban St. Louis to place on the market after his mother's passing, Franzen, in the autobiographical essay "House for Sale," "came to feel that the house had been my mother's novel, the concrete story she told about herself," its décor the record of an evolving stylistic sensibility that transformed the "cheap, homely department-store boilerplate" from which she'd begun into a "final draft" expressive of its maker. Even as he reframes her domestic artistry in the terms of his own craft, evoking an auteur who "added and replaced various passages as funds permitted," considered paintings' placement "like a writer pondering commas," traded early, rote palettes for "the true interior colors that she carried within her like a destiny," he marks, in his own strained reception of her masterwork, a filial betrayal.[8]

"What she wanted," in her youngest son's assessment, "was for you to come inside and feel embraced and delighted by what she'd made; she was showing you herself, by way of hospitality." Though he suspects his mother "would have experienced the devaluation" of her opus's eventual, below-asking sale price "as a dashing of her hopes, a rejection of her creative work, an unwelcome indication of her averageness," her sons' failure to attain her projected price only confirms, in monetary terms, their inability to "make ourselves want what we couldn't want." It's this aesthetic distance from her dated, traditional good taste, "the discomfort of how completely I'd outgrown the novel I'd once been so happy to live in," that feels, for Franzen, like "the big way I'd let her down."[9]

In *Purity*, this discomfort permeates the psyches of multiple co-protagonists. Paying a covert visit to his parents' East German dacha, Andreas Wolf imagines them "alone here on a winter Sunday, childless, their conversation infrequent and scarcely audible, in that older-couple way," and, under the tableau's influence, "felt his heart veer dangerously close to sympathy." Figured as a "massive block of granite at the center of her life," Pip Tyler's tenderness toward her own mother—that she "pitied her; suffered with her; warmed to the sound of her voice; felt an unsettling kind of nonsexual attraction to her body; was solicitous even of her mouth chemistry; wished her greater happiness; hated upsetting her; found her dear"—comes to seem "the problem," "the essence of the handicap she lived with; the presumable cause of her inability to be effective at anything."[10]

"It seemed" to Louis Holland "as if there were a specific organ in his brain which under extreme stimulus produced a sensation of love, more intense than any orgasm, but more dangerous too, because it was even less discriminate. A person could find himself loving enemies and homeless beggars and ridiculous parents, people from whom it had been so easy to live at a distance." Alongside these functions, the "specific organ" Louis describes would seem to serve as fiction's receptor, novels a route toward "eternal responsibility" for those whom "in a moment of weakness he allowed himself to love."[11] For Joey, as for Louis, fiction's promise—of a compassion accessed perspectivally, by entering "into each person's position"—is seen as posing a risk, or threat.

"I have never in my life," Jessica seethes, "felt so smalled and invisible and totally dissed" (*Freedom*, 357). Bemoaning a locale in which "the guys" surrounding her "are all either losers, jerks, or married" (357), she protests that "I think I'm at least worth five minutes of polite conversation. It's been eight months now, and I'm still waiting for those five minutes" (357–58). She's describing the frustrations of Manhattan's singles scene, but her remarks could as aptly apply to the role afforded her by *Freedom*.

Poor Jessica. "A working dog, not a show dog like Joey," she finds herself "devoted, like her father, to a declining and endangered and unprofitable enterprise"—the publishing industry—while her brother "gets rich almost effortlessly" by investing in shade-grown coffee "at exactly the moment when fortunes could be made in it," provided one has access to Connie's seed money, ill-gotten subcontractual dollars, and a parent's "South American connections" (533). The real Jessica—whom it "rankles" and "frustrates" to be passed over by parental favor, whom Joey's exploits "enrage and horrify" enough to rat him out, who gets "competitive," feels "envy"—is someone readers never encounter firsthand.

To see Jessica exalted as a "Genuinely Good Soul" (142), one "smitten with books, devoted to wildlife, talented at flute, stalwart as a babysitter, not so pretty as to be morally deformed by it, admired even by Merrie Paulsen" (8), is to witness a narrative flyover, an authorial dismissal no less firm for its niceness. In it, we may catch a narrative counterpart to the too-scrupulous politesse Richard directs toward those "whom he considered Good," may find the text's brief pretense to interest as "fake and condescending" as Walter does his friend's (134). We may whiff partiality when a similarly adoring description of Walter— who "not only knew about the Club of Rome and read difficult novels and appreciated Igor Stravinsky" but "could also sweat a copper pipe joint and do finish carpentry and identify birds by their songs and take good care of a problematic woman" (124)—proves not supporting character's summation but a protagonist's leading edge.

Likewise, Walter's ostensible compliment that "with Lalitha, what you saw was what you got" (489) perplexes when applied to a character of whom we glimpse so little. To observe that she is "not the worry and enigma and head-strong stranger that Patty, at some level, had always remained to him" (489) may be intimacy's testament for Walter but, for the Franzen narrator who worries enigmatic characters to life, signals disengagement. The novel allots to Lalitha seven words of backstory ("Indian. Bengali. She grew up in Missouri" [207]), a figure more than doubled if one includes Jessica's discovery that "apparently both her parents were engineers and never made a real meal in their lives" (353). The latter, "chilly, eccentric people, engineers, with strong accents," materialize in the wake of their daughter's untimely death, occasioning Walter's discomfort at the way "the mother kept erupting, loudly, unprovoked"— unprovoked?—"in a keening foreign wail" that "sounded strangely ceremonial and impersonal, like a lament for an idea" (554).

As a fiction writer, Franzen isn't the sort to sketch in an ethical grayscale whose every stroke captures a character's messy, imperfect humanity; instead, his novels arrive at the shading of complex characterization by layering heroic and villainous cels. For the revelation "that they were maybe not so different underneath" to propel a novel, the matchups must start out disparate indeed: Walter—in the tartly accurate assessment of Patty's sister Abigail—"Mr. Superhuman Good Guy Minnesotan Righteous Weirdo Naturelover" (521), Richard an unapologetic scoundrel who lauds, in Dylan, "the beautifully pure kind of asshole who made a young musician want to be an asshole himself" (132). Similarities between these two emerge gradually, via a narrative attentiveness spread unevenly among the novel's cast.

If Eliza ever gets into therapy, works the steps, reparents herself, learns how to have healthier relationships, it happens off-screen; if Jessica filches dues from her Amnesty International chapter or cheats on the GREs, we never hear; whatever deposits of anger, sorrow, disappointment underlie Dorothy's "eternally trusting niceness" (146), these remain unmined; who Lalitha might be, outside the metric that rates her "better than Patty" (304), goes unexplored.

Franzen's fiction trains readers to generate these loglines for characters whose on-page portraits, absent the perspectival detail provided by focal narration, remain mere caricatures, like the drawing, "half super-skilled and half clumsy and bad," presented to Patty by Eliza (52). "The way the player's body was low to the ground and violently slanting as she made a sharp turn," Patty notes, "was excellent, but the face and head were like some generic female in a first-aid booklet" (52). Indeed, the one-dimensionality of the text's sidelined women becomes a motif: Connie, in the narrator's assessment, "had no notion of wholeness" (11); "I'm not anybody" (276), Jenna self-abnegates; Abigail seems to Joey "like a sad cartoon version of his mother" (278); Patty concludes "that a certain kind of voice"—her own—"would do well to fall silent" (507).

When these characters' stories find expression in *Freedom*, they tend to enter the text not via narration but through the reluctantly attentive ear of Joey, whose role as "Designated Understander" expands throughout "2004." In response to Patty's "inappropriately frank" disclosures, he turns armchair therapist, evoking the enigmatic clinician who suggests she compose an autobiography: "'Why frightened?' he found himself saying, like Tony Soprano's shrink. 'Why guilty?'" (249). His aunt Abigail "mostly . . . delivered a monologue, with ironic commentary and self-conscious interjections, that was like a train that he was permitted to hop onto and ride for awhile" (278). "Once the door" to

Jenna's confidences "had opened even just a millimeter, once he'd slipped through the crack in it, he knew what to do. How to listen and how to understand. It wasn't fake listening or fake understanding, either. It was Joey in Womanland" (276). In this respect, he and Walter—who regards "the province of listening to women with sincere attentiveness" as "his turf," defended "fiercely" against Richard's encroachment (134)—may differ less than they appear.

Writing for *Harper's* in 1996, Franzen describes "human existence" as "defined by an Ache: the Ache of our not being, each of us, the center of the universe; of our desires forever outnumbering our means of satisfying them."[12] Informed by Connie that she has been having sex with her manager, Joey becomes aware that "the pain was quite extraordinary. And yet also weirdly welcome and restorative, bringing him news of his aliveness and his caughtness in a story larger than himself" (*Freedom*, 407). In the space-taking aftermath of this disclosure, he wonders "how there had come to be an ache named Connie at the center of his life," feels himself "driven crazy by so minutely feeling what she felt, by understanding her too well, by not being able to imagine her life without him" (408)—or his own, we might infer, without her.

"The problem," for Andy Aberant, "was love."[13] For Franzen, it's only as a last resort that love comes to be regarded as anything other than a problem: if his characters find their relationships necessary, saving, vital, they arrive at this conviction having first labeled connection and interdependence a liability, a weakness, a danger, an inconvenience, a risk. Introduced as a neighbor whom "it was in any case hard to resist" (*Freedom*, 5), Patty "couldn't help loving Joey just the way he was" (149); Joey, in turn, "liked her, in spite of everything; he couldn't help it" (244). With Connie, he wonders why, after years together, he was "being gripped, as if for the first time, by such a titanic undertow of *really liking her*," "feeling connected to her in such a scarily consequential way?" (257). "This is so unfair, you asshole," Walter cries, upon receiving a limited-release recording of *Songs for Walter* from his estranged best friend (557), who, himself, seems perplexed at Walter's having "slipped into his life before he'd shut the door on the world of ordinary people" (205).

In the autobiographical essay "My Bird Problem" (2005), Franzen trains on his own solipsist's calculus a self-scrutiny not unlike the gaze with which, as novelist, he regards foible-laden focal characters. After attending a talk about climate change by Al Gore, he shrugs off his distress during a thirty-minute crosstown stroll. Reassurance takes a characteristically apocalyptic form: the slim chance "that seawater from Greenland's melting ice cap would advance any farther than the Citarella market on Third Avenue, six blocks to the south and east," much less reach "my apartment . . . way up on the tenth floor." And yet: watching an insomniac's back-of-eyelid slideshow display "a desertified North America," Franzen confronts "the scenario I'd been at pains to avert for many years: not the world's falling apart in the future, but my feeling inconveniently obliged to care about it in the present." Where "not having kids" had once "freed me altogether" from personal investment in ecological catastrophe, he realizes that, despite his best efforts, "I couldn't find a way not to care about the billions of birds and thousands of avian species that were liable to be wiped out worldwide."[14]

This dilemma—the titular "problem"—joins other "news of his aliveness and his caughtness" in stories "larger than himself," which accumulate over the essay's course. Franzen "finally, sadly" concludes that "my ready-made escape route" from his relationship with the writer Kathy Chetkovich "had disappeared"; grieves the mother whom, after decades as a dutiful but ambivalent son, he had "finally started to love . . . near the end of her life"; succumbs to the "undefended sincerity" of birding; and accepts an attendant obligation "to know that something is doomed and to cheerfully try to save it anyway."[15]

In an essay about Kafka and autobiographical fiction, Franzen asserts that narrative "teaches us how to love ourselves even as we're being merciless toward ourselves; how to remain humane in the face of the most awful truths about ourselves." "It's not enough," he reiterates, "to love your characters, and it's not enough to be hard on your characters: you always have to try to be doing both at the same time." To do this—to craft protagonists who "are at once sympathetic subjects and dubious objects"—means "that you have to become a different person," one able "to write the next book," which itself requires "working on the story of your own life. Which is to say: your autobiography."[16]

As *Middlemarch* endeavors to do better than gossip can for Dorothea—whose remarriage her brother-in-law "never ceased to regard . . . as a mistake," who, according to local "tradition" among "those who had not seen anything of" the protagonist firsthand, "could not have been 'a nice woman'"[17] after all—*Freedom* commits to burrowing beneath its protagonists' "nicey-nice surface[s]," exploring areas of moral complexity between or beyond binary assessments of the good people they wish to be, the bad people they fear they are.

Nowhere is this more true than in *MISTAKES*. Witnessing Patty's surrender to her messiest impulses—to sleep with her husband's best friend, to snub her daughter and smother her son, to get wasted and slash her neighbor's snow tires, to become, "for all her choices and all her freedom," only "more miserable" (*Freedom*, 181), while acknowledging "her wish to be a good person" (158), someone who "worked hard to be a great mom and homemaker" (147), who finds her way to a "wretchedly paid but otherwise nearly ideal job" (510) imparting to middle-school athletes "the total dedication and tough love and lessons in teamwork that her own coaches once gave her" (531)—readers see the protagonist become "a third thing: a flickering consciousness, a simultaneity of culpable urge and poignant self-reproach, a person in process."[18] More than that, though: we watch as Patty sees herself in, and sees herself through, this becoming.

Patty's happy ending, like that of "My Bird Problem," resembles détente. In *MISTAKES WERE MADE (CONCLUSION)*, subtitled "A Sort of Letter to Her Reader by Patty Berglund," the autobiographer returns to document the six-year marital hiatus she devotes to a list of long-deferred yet pressing tasks: "to develop a career and a more solid post-athletic identity, get some experience with other kinds of men, and generally acquire more maturity" (*Freedom*, 118), or, more succinctly put, "figure out some decent and satisfying way to live" (181). In a paradox perhaps appropriate to this autobiography, her first onward steps backtrack: returning to her parents' home during Ray's final months, "Patty sat with her father, held his hand, and allowed herself to love him," in response to which "she could almost physically feel her emotional organs rearranging themselves, bringing her self-pity plainly into view at last, in its full obscenity, like a hideous purple-red growth in her that needed to be cut out" (513).

On the far side of this epiphany, Patty—"who will always be competitive" (514); whom "nobody will ever mistake . . . for a pillar of resolve and dignity" (509); whose "dream of creating a fresh life, entirely from scratch, independent, had been just that: a dream" (514); who, "although she wants to become a better person in every way" (534) and "believes herself to be genuinely changed, and doing infinitely better than in the old days" (507), has "sadly begun to realize that this ideal may very well be unattainable" (534)—appears at once profoundly altered, amusingly similar, emphatically in process.

6

THE MORE HE FOUGHT ABOUT IT,
THE ANGRIER HE GOT

For nearly thirty years, Franzen has been telling the same story: not—or not only—the multigenerational Midwestern saga with its rigid or rudderless parents, its children messily fledging, but another story, about fiction.

In 1996, speaking on a televised roundtable about the "Future of American Fiction," Franzen sketched a culture in which "people who read books, who seriously read books, who read a lot of books, nowadays, are just like a priori not of the mainstream," such that novelists address "a weird audience who is defined in large part by their nonparticipation in mass entertainments of that kind." This stands in contrast to "a golden hundred years before TV and movies had fully taken over," during which "the novel was the only game." "So, what," cuts in David Foster Wallace, Franzen's poptimistic copanelist on the segment, "the only people who read, like, serious fiction are people who don't watch TV?"[1]

Construing the readership for fiction as a counterculturally backward-looking bunch who yearn for *antan* with its deeper, downier *nieges*, Franzen commits in turn "to just basically keep on doing the same old kind of book, making little subtle nods to the fact that it's now 1996 and not 1896."[2]

As he wrote that year in *Harper's*, *The Twenty-Seventh City*'s limelit media junket, modest compared with those that were to follow, had taught Franzen that "the money, the hype, the limo ride to a *Vogue* shoot weren't fringe benefits" but "the main prize, the consolation for no longer mattering to a culture." *Strong Motion* cemented his certainty that "there was *no* place in the world for fiction writers."[3]

There were, though: places, plural. With the appearance of *The Corrections*, there was space for Franzen on the chaises of Oprah Winfrey and Terry Gross, in the columns of Michiko Kakutani's *Times* copy, on best of-the-aughts lists and in the dissertations of freshly minted PhDs. Bookstores made room, provided lecterns to prop up the tome and microphones to project Franzen's sonorous, pause-laden speech; rows of chairs from which audience Qs would issue, to which authorial As would be addressed; square footage through which signing lines could snake. There were spots on the calendars, and in the armchairs, of readers who paged solo and book groups that congregated to discuss. Library shelves opened a gap in PS3556 and 813 to house the plastic-slickered hardbacks. The Pulitzer shortlist, the National Book Award's dais—these, too, welcomed him.

Asked by the author Donald Antrim, in 2001, what "large preoccupations" might arc across his career, Franzen named "the sense of being a threatened writer with a threatened sense of importance, and therefore a threatened sense of personhood." "From my perspective," he expands, "I feel like I'm part of an embattled, retreating cultural minority," one "that cares about books and about the values that have been traditionally associated with literature."[4]

To coincide with *Freedom*'s 2010 release, Franzen stared dolefully out from *Time*'s August 23 issue. "The magazine whose red border twice enclosed the face of James Joyce," whose shift over his lifetime's course from featuring Baldwin and Cheever to Turow and King had signaled, in *Harper's*, the novel's decline, now showed Franzen. "Great American Novelist," the cover's header pronounced.[5]

The same week, while vacationing with his family on Martha's Vineyard, Barack Obama procured an advance reader's copy of *Freedom* from Bunch of Grapes Bookstore, along with copies of *To Kill a Mockingbird* and Steinbeck's *The Red Pony*; the shopping trip itself reached national news outlets. In October, the president—who, in an interview with the novelist Marilynne Robinson, would later reflect that "when I think about how I understand my role as citizen . . . the most important stuff I've learned I think I've learned from novels"—hosted Franzen at the White House.[6]

Upon *Purity*'s publication in 2015, Franzen told the *Financial Times* that "I am literally, in terms of my income, a 1 per center," but "I spend my time connected to the poverty that's fundamental to mankind, because I'm a fiction writer." "I'm a poor person who has money," he dared add.[7]

"How did a person so extremely fortunate," muses Franzen, "become the Great Hater?" It's his central query for Karl Kraus, the fin-de-siècle Viennese satirist, and a fair question for this bilious U.S. novelist of a latter *siècle*'s *fin*. "I was a white male heterosexual American with good friends and perfect health," he tallies, "and yet, for all my privileges, I became an extremely angry person."[8]

So, not yet; because, not despite. "I wonder if he was so angry," Franzen hazards, of Kraus, "*because* he was so privileged." The essayist's "anger," in Franzen's diagnosis, "relieved some of the discomfort of his own privilege, by reassuring him that he was also a victim," satisfying his yearning, "like any artist . . . to be an individual" via "a violent shrugging-off of categories that threatened his individual integrity," of which "his privilege" was "just one."[9]

In *Middlemarch*, Eliot observes that "we all of us, grave or light, get our thoughts entangled in metaphors, and act fatally on the strength of them."[10] Strike "act" in favor of "reason" or "persuade," and it could serve as a one-line review of Franzen's first essay collection, *How to Be Alone* (2002), a disaster-tourist's trip through "the anxious mid-nineties" (165) and no-calmer early aughts. Alongside pieces on private prisons' rise, the decline of public space, postal-service dysfunction, big tobacco's clout, three of the collection's contents—"The Reader in Exile" (1995), "Scavenging" (1996), and "Why Bother?" (1996)—form a rough triptych on the adversarial relationship their author proposes between readership and technological change. Each issues from a particular brush with obsolescence: Franzen's decision to bin his Sony Trinitron television set because, "as long as it was in the house . . . I wasn't reading books"; his discovery of the telephone model he then used, a circa-1982 "basic black AT&T rotary," in a museum case; and "the decline of the broad-canvas novel."[11]

The pieces in this trio perform a series of autopsies, surveying contemporary culture like a procedural's corpse-dense morgue: "the camera drove a stake through the heart of serious portraiture, television has killed the novel of social reportage," and, "for every reader who dies today, a viewer is born." Their voice adopts the dire tones of a Clinton-era Cassandra, "witnessing . . . the final tipping of a balance" between words' and images' primacy, the novel "teetering on the brink" of irrelevance, "each reader and writer an island" against "the rising waters of electronic culture." Franzen's prose conjures legions of "professional book critics, who ought to be the front line of the novel's defenders" yet haven't "raised the alarm," instead fleeing the field where one review's subject, Sven Birkerts, stands alone, "a loyal soldier deserted by his regiment," his *Gutenberg Elegies* playing a "brave but plaintive" taps for fiction's lost repute.[12]

The "Quest stands upon the edge of a knife. Stray but a little and it will fail, to the ruin of all": we might be Mordor-bound, almost.[13] Franzen deploys a series of oppositional, often martial metaphors for persuasive effect; they draft him as well. The promising young novelist of protocurmudgeonly mien doesn't stay tapping at his Smith-Corona while the camera vampire-slays serious portraiture and Sven Birkerts perishes at Ypres. Figuring contemporary culture as a series of ominous forces threatening to overwhelm the novel—a flood, an onslaught, an authoritarian regime—transforms the novelist, too: into the levee holding digital deluge at bay, the lonely soldier posing in silhouette, the suffragette exploding postboxes in art's defense. For the younger Franzen, *The Twenty-Seventh City* had served as a means of "sending my bombs in a Jiffy-Pak mailer of irony and understatement," while *Strong Motion* let him "come out throwing rhetorical Molotov cocktails."[14] These descriptions sketch the fiction writer as a solitary subversive beset by elementally larger and more powerful foes, a rhetorical position to which figurative language has given Franzen access throughout his career.

A metaphor's power doesn't reside only in the device's ability to transform tenor into vehicle but its vehicle's potential to port readers and writers alike into its world, to recast their relations to the tenor and reshape the conversation's terms. The truism that skillful writers "extend" their metaphors, while verbal klutzes "mix" one with another, expresses the metaphor's authority as an artist's responsibility—to stay in the metaphor's universe, to "yes-and" an initial similarity one observes.

The "media landscape," as scoped from the vantage of Franzen's essays, resembles a battlefield, arterially entrenched, hilled with shell-holes, tined by the stripped, strafed trunks of what might, once, have been trees. In such environs, newer technologies assume opponents' fixed positions, menacing those that obsolesce: "a rotary phone . . . still served proudly in my living room," a campaign-proven veteran affront-ing "the regiments of tasteful black boxes billeted in every house across the land."[15]

When a critic-slash-novelist stations critics in a combat zone and summarizes his narrative résumé as a series of incendiary devices, those figures reframe the discussion, borrowing for his argument the parameters, stakes, assumptions of military engagements. Everyone in dialogue with such a speaker doesn't necessarily turn combatant; unless they take care, though, they may all begin describing a war, adapting their verbal habitus to fit that situation. They might, for instance, find them-selves taking on a heightened, solemn register; adopting the blunt polarities of us-them, good-evil, winner-loser; ascribing life-or-death importance to scenarios that don't carry mortal risk.[16] So comprehensive are military metaphors—so totalizing is war—that even an attempt to opt out of these rhetorical positions can come to resemble a charged, morally consequential stance. Refusal to join Franzen in the vanguard he designates or to embed with his unit as a correspondent dispatching from the front might be construed as an act of pacifism, bystanding, desertion.

Should a writer purport to have placed "a declaration of literary inde-pendence in *Harper's*," readers who have absorbed America's cultural myths are asked to see the statement's author as a patriotic upstart, to sort all parties swiftly onto two sides of a conflict that pits revolutionary youth against tyrannical loyalists of the old order. Over a career, the critic who understands "the role of the essayist as a firefighter, whose job, while everyone else is fleeing the flames of shame, is to run straight into them," may learn to address every situation in the tones and tempi of emergency, may dull his ability to see the world except in terms of so many arsonists, so much dry tinder.[17]

Nowhere are the consequences of this tendency—the firefighter's to identify, in every event, an active or potential blaze—more evident than in "Why Bother?," often referred to as "the *Harper's* Essay" after the venue in which it originally appeared, to sensation, as "Perchance to Dream" (1996). A portrait of the author's "despair about the American novel," "Why Bother?" issues from the perspective of a working novelist and lifelong reader who sees the social novel as increasingly imperiled—by television, consumerism, and modernity more broadly construed—and fears thereby losing his own sense of connection with literary community and culture. If "depression presents itself as a realism regarding the rottenness of the world in general and . . . your life in particular," the narrative of grievance is the means by which Franzen's "Ache" attempts to assume logic's form, and metaphor becomes its mechanism for doing so. Steeped in a "feeling of oppositionality" that transforms firing squads into mere vehicles and "simply picking up a novel after dinner" into "a kind of cultural *Je refuse!*," the *Harper's* Essay attests to the persuasive power and, with it, the deceptive potential of the figures formed by Franzen's as-ifness.[18]

Of these, perhaps most prominent is a passage describing U.S. literary culture as a Midwestern cityscape.[19] After publishing *The Twenty-Seventh City*, Franzen's vision of "literary America . . . bore a strange resemblance to the St. Louis I'd grown up in: a once-great city that had been gutted and drained by white flight and superhighways" (*How to Be Alone*, 62).[20] He positions as squatters or arrivistes the "ethnic and cultural enclaves" of marginalized writers who "had taken over the structures vacated by fleeing straight white males" (62), sees the resulting city as "once-great," "depressed," and "underemployed," its "few still-vital cultural monuments"—in deference, apparently, to visiting "suburban readers" (H)—"well-policed" (62). Franzen's own analogue, if anywhere in this metaphorical metro area, appears to reside among the "few city-loving artists" who, "attracted to the diversity and grittiness that only a city can offer" (H), "continued to hole up in old warehouses" (62). His description reflects the blinkered perspective of a white writer who, as he put it in 2017, "was aesthetically attracted to cities but morbidly afraid of being shot," who ceased being "afraid of the city" only when "I could go downtown and safely walk with my friends on the alphabet streets, which were being colonized by young white people."[21]

"Why Bother?" takes audible solace in the possibility, voiced by Don DeLillo, that "if the social novel lives, but only barely, surviving in the cracks and ruts of culture, maybe it will be taken more seriously, as an endangered spectacle." Franzen feels "a surge of hope" in response to DeLillo's postscript: "if serious reading dwindles to near nothingness," "the thing we're talking about when we use the word 'identity' has reached an end." In that scenario, Franzen imagines that "if multiculturalism succeeds in making us a nation of independently empowered tribes, each tribe will be deprived the comfort of victimhood." Yet "the comfort of victimhood" is precisely what these essays set out to invent from whole cloth, claiming membership in "this marginalized community" of writers and readers whose "pursuit of substance in a time of ever-increasing evanescence" Franzen equates to experiences of structural oppression. The "*Je refuse*" he lodges emerges as refusal "to settle for (and thereby participate in) your own marginalization as a writer, to accept as inevitable a shrinking audience," a dissent that takes—as his imagined marginalization does—figurative form.[22]

Where did the self-pity come from? The inordinate volume of it? By almost any standard, Jonathan Franzen *led a luxurious life. He had all day every day to figure out some decent and satisfying way to live, and yet all he ever seemed to get for all his choices and all his freedom was more miserable. The* critic *is almost forced the conclusion that* Jonathan Franzen *pitied himself for being so free (Freedom, 181).*

In *The Great War and Modern Memory*, Paul Fussell identifies a "system of 'high' diction," the specific style of verbal militarism that was "not the least of the ultimate casualties of [the First World War]." He proposes to "set out this 'raised,' essentially feudal language in a table of equivalents," a complex system of morally laden euphemism in which "the draft-notice is *the summons*," "one's death is one's *fate*," "dead bodies constitute *ashes*, or *dust*." If the language of war lost this heightened, solemn form, it was superseded by a new martial argot that permeated the broader culture. Long after the First World War, ex- and noncombatants alike retained "its special diction and system of metaphor, its whole jargon of techniques and tactics and strategy," which, "even if now attenuated and largely metaphorical . . . resides everywhere just below the surface of modern experience." Fussell notes that "one says, 'We were bombarded with forms' or 'We've had a barrage of complaints today' without, of course, any sharp awareness that one is recalling war and yet with a sense that such figures are appropriate to the modern situation."[23]

In her 1989 essay "AIDS and Its Metaphors," Susan Sontag calls "future-mindedness . . . the distinctive mental habit, and corruption, of [the twentieth] century." As statistical modeling has become more sophisticated, providing fodder for extrapolation toward projected outcomes, she argues, "anything in history or nature that can be described as changing steadily can be seen as heading toward catastrophe," bifurcating awareness into "what is happening now" and "what it portends: the imminent, but not yet actual, and not really graspable, disaster." Sontag's argument traces these corrosive ethical and perceptual effects to "the taste for worst-case scenarios," which, whether as a line of reasoning or the rhetorical style and linguistic figures that accompany it, "expresses an imaginative complicity with disaster. The sense of cultural distress or failure gives rise to the desire for a clean sweep, a tabula rasa. No one wants a plague, of course. But, yes, it would be a chance to begin again. And beginning again—that is very modern, very American, too."[24]

Central to the rhetoric of apocalypse, in Sontag's analysis, are metaphors, which "cannot be distanced just by abstaining from them. They have to be exposed, criticized, belabored, used up." Of these, she finds most distasteful and distortive "the military metaphor," which, in licensing a "total war" on its opponent, "overmobilizes" and "overdescribes." "We are not," she corrects, "being invaded. The body is not a battlefield. The ill are neither unavoidable casualties nor the enemy. We—medicine, society—are not authorized to fight back by any means whatever." And, as for "that metaphor, the military one": Sontag urges her audience to "give it back to the warmakers."[25]

Franzen's reliance on the persuasive tactics Sontag cautions against stand out in a passage from the *Harper's* Essay. In *Catch-22*, the younger Franzen had identified "a model for an uncompromising novel that had found a big audience," its success based on its author's having "figured out a way of outdoing the actuality, employing the illogic of modern warfare as a metaphor for the more general denaturing of American reality." Following Heller's lead, he began his career with the proposition that "a novelist could trick Americans into confronting" their culture's unpalatable realities "if only he could package his subversive bombs in a sufficiently seductive narrative."[26]

However soberly he vows to separate himself from the "critics inclined to alarmism," for whom "the shift from a culture based on the printed word to a culture based on virtual images . . . feels apocalyptic," Franzen succumbs to the doomsayer's El Doradan quest for "a killer argument that will make the imminence of apocalypse self-evident." His own attempt at death-by-thesis opens with the object lesson of retiring his television, a Sony Trinitron whose spotty reception and "wood-look veneer" might have aroused his sympathy had they described a hi-fi. The set, however, "had to go, because as long as it was in the house, reachable by some combination of extension cords, I wasn't reading books." Its departure signals the gallant's reluctant side-taking in a catastrophic "toss-up" between "living without electronic access to my country's culture" and "trying to survive in that culture without the self-definition I get from regular immersion in literature."[27]

"One day the victim of the market," he extrapolates, "turns out not to be a trivial thing, like a rotary phone or a vinyl disc, but a thing of life-and-death importance to me, like the literary novel." To the Mercer Museum's display of obsolescent devices, imagination affixes a case for fiction, now just another "of the tools that American industrialization was rendering useless," defunct triple-deckers stacked like slabs atop eight-track tapes, Franzen's treasured "copies of Singer and Gaddis and O'Connor" utterly discarded, "as on the ash-heap of history."[28]

❖ ❖ ❖

Not that a person who spends four years and forty thousand words accounting for his relationship with Jonathan Franzen's fiction should, necessarily, offer any opinion on the codependent pains Franzen takes to accommodate his rotary phone.

Narrators more reliable than himself on the subject of Jonathan Franzen approached eight billion; they spanned seven Terran continents, bobbed on water, sailed through air, orbited Earth. There were those disinclined toward, and those indifferent to, and those unaware of Jonathan Franzen; there were those without Franzenward tendencies, those with Franzenward tendencies they felt no call to mull, and those who, if they examined their Franzenward tendencies, never *became aware, in a word, of codependency,* who *continued to cover for* nothing that was *losing its ability to cope with the modern world* (*How to Be Alone*, 196).

It wasn't difficult, for instance, to identify interlocutors for Franzen who'd never extolled the virtues of the toaster—an antediluvian Sunbeam Radiant Control—that charred bread and smoked when left plugged in; who were no longer, at time of writing, toting an iPod Nano; who had been described as a "notorious Luddite" by zero of their intimates. Such people didn't cling to their copy of *Farther Away* as ballast, *because* they *loved it and* were *afraid of change,* or, if they chanced to do this, they stopped short of declaring authorial obsolescence a *character defect* of Franzen's while knowing well enough that *the defect, the disease,* inhered *in* them (*How to Be Alone*, 196–97).

❖ ❖ ❖

"God was dead: to begin with," opens Ali Smith's novel *Winter*, the second in her Seasonal Quartet. An inventory follows: "And romance was dead. Chivalry was dead. Poetry, the novel, painting, they were all dead, and art was dead. Theater and cinema were both dead. Literature was dead. The book was dead. Modernism, postmodernism, realism and surrealism were all dead. Jazz was dead, pop music, disco, rap, classical music, dead. Culture was dead." From this catalogue of expressive forms, the narrator's list extends to encompass political systems, abstract concepts, ethical values, digital platforms. While a few concepts evade, thus far, the general die-off—"life," for instance, "wasn't yet dead. Revolution wasn't dead. Racial equality wasn't dead. Hatred wasn't dead"—these exceptions soon spark further enumeration: "But the computer? Dead. TV? Dead. Radio? Dead."[29]

"The death of the novel," that commonplace of every-so-often essays in arts sections and literary reviews, is, of course, itself a metaphor. Novels' nearest approach to sentience is vicarious or parasitic—as a pastime of writers and readers who lend them vital hours; their decease, equally figurative. If, in its fortress of "cultural authority," the novel ails, its sickness resembles the Fisher King's: an enchantment of the sort that sours soil, rots produce, turns dairy, scatters game. Called so often to fiction's bedside, one might be tempted by the form's "curiously bad health" to adopt the brisk tone of Lady Bracknell, find "this shilly-shallying with the question . . . absurd," declare it "high time" that Franzen "make up his mind" whether the novel, like Algie's invented, perpetually unwell acquaintance Mr. Bunbury, "was going to live or die."[30]

Where they once passed out of use, like a gadget, the novels in Franzen's essays have begun, more recently, to go extinct, like a species. Despite substitutions of tenor and, finally, of vehicle, though, the structure of his comparisons has remained, for decades, remarkably stable. Combining grief journal, travelogue, and literary history, the essay "Farther Away" (2011) espies the "rise of the novel," in Ian Watt's titular phrase, through a naturalist's lens, such that early canons become "leading specimens of the form . . . collected in authoritative sets," like lepidopterists' pinnings, and authors themselves turn taxonomist, as when Henry Fielding terms his characters "species" to suggest "something more than individual, less than universal." "Walking on [the island,]

Robinson, looking for delicate endemic ferns at the blackberry's margins," the author "began to see the novel as an organism that had mutated, on the island of England, into a virulent invasive that then spread from country to country until it conquered the planet."[31]

"The blackberry on Robinson Crusoe Island," he analogizes, "was like the conquering novel, yes, but it seemed to me no less like the Internet, that BlackBerry-borne invasive, which, instead of mapping the self onto a narrative, maps the self onto the world," producing "the even more virulent and even more radically individualistic invader that is now displacing the novel and its offspring." Having "proliferated subgenerically into movies and TV shows and late-model video games," fiction "has so thoroughly transformed" our modes of narrative engagement "that the thing itself is at risk of no longer being needed." As "the Masafueran species requires undisturbed native fern forest, and its population, never large, appears to be declining" because of "predation by invasive rats and cats," so distraction fragments the tracts of silence and solitude that nurture fiction's reception, putative readers picked off by bingeable watches and notification badges' dopamine hits.[32]

In his 2016 essay collection *The End of the End of the Earth*, the novel all but ceases to act as tenor in his system of metaphors, but that system remains strikingly consistent in other respects. These essays' *age d'or* is "the Miocene epoch, when birds ruled the planet." "The other world-dominating animals that evolution has produced" (40), "the former rulers of the natural realm," avian life provides "our last, best connection to a natural world that is otherwise receding." In the face of climate change, "every one of us is now in the position of the indigenous Americans when the Europeans arrived with guns and smallpox."[33] As in the essays of *Harper's*-era Franzen, analogy engineers a misplaced sense of equivalence between experiences and levels vast disparities in structural privilege, eliding the role unevenly allocated wealth and power play in distributing the harshest consequences of climate catastrophe.

"That even an apocalypse can be made to seem part of the ordinary horizon of expectation," Sontag asserts, "constitutes an unparalleled violence that is being done to our sense of reality, to our humanity."[34] And yet: in *The Great Derangement*, Amitav Ghosh examines another sort of "violence . . . done to our sense of reality, to our humanity," as Sontag might term it, by the refusal—in culture broadly construed but particularly in the "realist" or "literary" novel of bourgeois life—to acknowledge apocalypse when it exists well within the ordinary horizon of expectation.

As residents of "a time when the wild has become the norm," during which extreme weather events, however "improbable" they might be, "are neither surreal nor magical" but "overwhelmingly, urgently, astoundingly real," our novelists, in Ghosh's account, will be found to have furthered "the modes of concealment that prevented people from recognizing the realities of their plight." Ghosh sees the realist novel as a narrative analog of the hubris-fueled colonial architectures whose "complacency . . . was itself a kind of madness." The roots of this abdication on literary realism's part lie, Ghosh argues, in the intellectual, historical, and political soil that fed the novel's formal development, particularly the rise of statistics and probabilities as a mode of sense making, which coincided with the novel's "banishing of the improbable and the insertion of the everyday." Given literary fiction's dearth of storytelling tools for representing extraordinary events—however commonplace they become—Ghosh projects that, as climate catastrophe intensifies, "the mansion of serious fiction, like the doomed waterfront properties of Mumbai and Miami Beach, will double down on its current sense of itself, building ever higher barricades to keep the waves at bay."[35]

The frustrations and contradictions of Franzen's oeuvre emblematically illustrate the tendencies Ghosh observes. At the level of form and content, Franzen has been centrally "preoccupied with the unreal, willfully self-deceptive worlds we make for ourselves to live in," has spent decades acting as cartographer to his characters' countless attempts to circumambulate and their eventual collisions with unavoidable actualities.[36] Despite this, his has been a career spent shoring up the walls—indeed, we might call them battlements—of what Ghosh terms "the mansion of serious fiction," attempting to "double down" on the novel's "current sense of itself," in defiance of climatological crises whose improbability renders them no less real.

As a novelist, Franzen aims skepticism at the same lines of reasoning his essays sometimes succumb to. Working toward her MFA, *Purity*'s Leila Helou encounters the novelist Charles Blenheim at the "apex" of a career—and an ecosystem of literary accolades—that delivers "a Lannan Fellowship year and a front-page *Times* review," styles him "the heir of John Barth and Stanley Elkin." Feted thus for *Mad Sad Dad*, an actually "great book"—as in, "hilarious," "gorgeous"—Charles has "settled down to write the *big book*, the novel that would secure him his place in the modern American canon." Whereas, "once upon a time, it had sufficed to write *The Sound and the Fury* or *The Sun Also Rises* . . . now bigness was essential. Thickness, length."[37]

Bigness—of repute, of appetite, of frame—also shapes his alpha-predatory appeal to Leila. "As if he were a big cat and she, with her slightness, her littleness, the mouse on which he compulsively pounced," their relationship unfolds in a nature-documentary "drama" that yowls with "the pouncing, the bouncing, the screaming of the prey." Peak implies downslope: authorial unsuccess's entrée reveals the *big book* as "bloated and immensely disagreeable," its progenitor a pantherine nuisance who transforms Leila's "little apartment on Capitol Hill" to "the sour-smelling cage of a big cat too depressed to groom itself."[38]

Satire shreds Charles's Great American Novelist—as it does the avant-garde filmmaker of Anabel, the novel's other significant ex—resizing to the texture of subplots' fill the "bigness" of *Mad Sad Dad*'s po-mo bro cachet, the allotted "hour for each day of the lunar month" in Anabel's debut. So smallened, they serve as fodder for the dysfunctional first acts of Leila and Tom Aberant, two journalists whose working styles—brass-tacked, nonsenseless, hypercompetent—produce daily dispatches as brisk and factual as their former spouses' are navel-gazingly overwrought. At the *Denver Independent*, stories, if they achieve "bigness," arrive there not via an auteur's vision but through diffuser processes of sourced attribution, editorial oversight, collaborative research.

Like Anabel—who sets out to compose an exhaustive filmic self-portrait of pointillist one-centimeter squares only to be "paralyzed by jealousy" of her newsman husband's "smaller but completable" feats of reportage—Charles nurses "an undercurrent of resentment" at Leila's "ability to perform household tasks while managing, in her flat reportorial way, to string a few paragraphs together."[39] That she does so in "the small scrap of time when she was free to toil on her scratchings, at the child-size desk of his older daughter" (198), illustrates the covetous eye *Purity*'s *big book* turns toward smallness, the contempt it reserves for the species of self-aggrandizing artistic spectacle it most resembles.

More and more, it appeared that *the actual root cause of* Franzen's *stupidity was* his *wish for* the reader *to keep on being* his *little boy-pal: to continue being more entertained and fascinated by his* novels *than by great TV or* any other narrative form. *This was the sick heart of* his *dumbness:* he *was* competing (*Freedom*, 247).

As these metaphors multiply across Franzen's career, so they reproduce themselves in conversations about his work. A defense—like Lev Grossman's cover feature for *Time*, in 2010—often accedes to Franzen by adopting his preferred metaphors, shoring up the rhetorical positions he has sought to occupy. Surveying sea otters at a Moss Landing estuary, Grossman casts Franzen as "a member of another perennially threatened species, the American literary novelist," who yet remains "one of contemporary fiction's great populists and a key ally of the beleaguered modern reader." The Oprah debacle was "a public mugging." In contrast to the "literary megafauna" of DeLillo-aligned postmodern authors and aughts-era fiction that "zoomed deep in, exploring subcultures, individual voices, specific ethnic communities," Franzen widens his lens to produce "the all-embracing, way-we-live-now novel," which his latest, with "an unshowy, almost egoless perfection," typifies: "*Freedom* isn't about a subculture; it's about the culture. It's not a microcosm; it's a cosm." His "predecessors" are "Bellow and Mailer and Updike," while "Fitzgerald and Hemingway" provide an analog for his friendship with David Foster Wallace.[40]

Regarding technique, the paean-as-profile aphorizes that "a writer has to be both boxer and trainer at the same time, and Franzen's trainer is a hard-ass." "His attitude toward his characters is tender but ruthless," goes one of Grossman's similes, "like that of a man who loves his horse but has no choice to put it down," assigning the lyrical stoicism of a Cormac McCarthy–esque machismo to someone whose self-styled masculinity comprises more elder-statesmanlike sententiousness, nebbishy self-scrutiny, pugilistic pique. During the birding jaunt near-obligatory in magazine profiles of Franzen, Grossman, offered his subject's binoculars to peer at a plover, concedes that "even I . . . can see that it's a hell of a bird, with its solid breastplate of black feathers," and it transforms into a little bruiser, part hoplite, as seen by Raymond Chandler; the sea otters, "if they could talk . . . would tell Franzen to man up."[41]

If Grossman's awestruck tone falters, it's with the assessment that Franzen, "singularly ungifted at what you might call brand management, which for better or worse has become part of the writer's job in these late, decadent days," makes for "a terrible politician."[42] Even glancing acquaintance with his literary niche dispels any notion of a public-facing Franzen universally beloved or imbued with bonhomie. Interviewing him in 2015, Terry Gross expressed surprise at the author photo for *Purity*—in which a radiant Franzen stands, pants cuffed, in surf—by matter-of-factly remarking that "happy-looking is not the first description that comes to mind when people think of you."[43] If successful brand management consists of an author's associating with their brand qualities like tact, collegiality, graciousness, then Franzen is "ungifted at . . . brand management" indeed.[44]

In *How to Do Nothing* (2019), an invitingly expansive book-length essay about technology's pervasive influence and the curative properties of, among other practices, birding—one not, mercifully, by Franzen— Jenny Odell describes the difference between the bespoke "Jenny mix" digitally generated by a streaming service and a radio station curated by live DJ. "An algorithmic 'honing in,'" she writes, "would seem to incrementally entomb me as an ever-more stable image of what I like and why," one's personal brand reducible to "a reliable, unchanging pattern of snap judgments: 'I like this' and 'I don't like this,' with little room for ambiguity or contradiction."[45]

Through Odell's lens, Franzen's brand—memorably described by Nicholas Dames as the "Obsolete Realist"[46]—clarifies into one of the sturdiest in contemporary literature: the sort of opinion Jonathan

Franzen would hold, the kind of thing he might say or do, is easily imagined; his gaffes and dust-ups visible, remarked upon, well beyond the audience of his fiction. Like the sequence of upvotes and down-votes algorithmically distillable to the ideal "Jenny mix," Franzen's stances are nothing if not clear, predictable, stable over time. In turn, he evokes strong sentiments; as Chuck Klosterman puts it, "the deeper explanation for Franzen's import is something that's hard to quantify but easy to feel: For whatever reason, people just care about him *more*. They love him more, they criticize him more, and they think about him more."[47]

In a 2002 interview, Franzen spoke about his construction of "a public me" "much smarter than me, and much more together than me" for the nonfiction pieces subsequently compiled as *How to Be Alone*. The statement that "I construct an I" isn't, per se, revealing: even the most confessionally inclined essayist must negotiate some distance between a lived and written self. More striking is his account of the process by which Franzen—self-described as "a mess in my day-to-day life," "quite inarticulate"—renders these essays' first-person voice. "A mess" means, for Franzen's purposes, prone to "think one thing one morning and the opposite the next," while "quite inarticulate" refers to the verbal signatures of ambivalence, the " 'like,' and 'sort of,' and 'in a way' " that provide release valves for opinions' pressure.[48]

Throughout Franzen's life in public, beginning with the *Harper's* Essay, he has figured himself as embattled, enemy-beset. The metaphors he uses are powerful; most conversations about him enter their universe—accept, even in disagreement, their terms. The oppositional framing of Franzen's career—the opinions Franzen holds, his means of expressing them, the positions they invite others to take with respect to his work and persona—flatten nuance, entrench stances, limit exchange. As with Odell's sequence of "snap judgements," they "leave little room for ambiguity or contradiction" and, over time, stand to "incrementally entomb" many conversations about Franzen and—perhaps most of all—the author himself.

According to a long and very unflattering story he'd assembled from the author's nonfiction dossier, Franzen *had made quite a mess of his professional life* as an essayist. *His* reader *had some difficulty reconciling* this Franzen—*arrogant, high-handed, ethically compromised—with the* measured, ambivalent novelist *he remembered* describing the Lamberts and Berglunds so sympathetically. *It seemed strange that* Franzen, *who* reviled the internet *and whose* preference *was* for third-person prose, *should he in trouble now for* click-baiting readers *and* interring himself in an inflexible "I." *Then again, there had always been something not quite right about* Jonathan Franzen (*Freedom*, 3).

"Radio: now that's a medium I can get behind," rhapsodizes Frank Navasky, a columnist in Nora Ephron's film *You've Got Mail*, who dreams of writing about "something really relevant for today, like the Luddite movement in nineteenth-century England." Forgetting his name, one character calls to mind "that nut from the *Observer*, the one who's so in love with his typewriter," a contraption called the Olympia Report Deluxe Electric—that's "'report,' as in gunshot," he gushes. The precision of the script's satire lances Navasky's provocative, metaphor-replete defense of the indie bookstore at the film's center: "If this precious resource is killed by the cold cash cow of Foxbooks," he bloviates, its closure will portend "the end of Western civilization as we know it"—as will computerized solitaire, according to his lines in the film's opening scene.[49]

In *The Friend*, Sigrid Nunez's narrator rehearses the "various gripes" of the novel's unnamed addressee, a writer who has killed himself, leaving his Great Dane in her care: while living, he'd lamented "how books were dying, literature was dying," how "no novel, no matter how brilliantly written or full of ideas, was going to have any meaningful effect on society, when it was impossible to imagine anything like" the scene of Abraham Lincoln's 1862 meeting with Harriet Beecher Stowe.[50] "Haven't you wondered," mansplains a louche party guest in Natasha Lyonne's series *Russian Doll*, "why visual art no longer carries the weight it did thirty years ago?" "I've literally never wondered that," his addressee responds.[51] If Franzen's self-conception resembles, in Frank Navasky's words, "a lone reed, standing tall, waving boldly in the corrupt sands of commerce," each of these texts has its own method of sidestepping the pompousness and polarity of that persona.[52]

If Grossman overlooks the "missteps" that, for Parul Sehgal, mar Franzen's early career—"the satirist's blind spot for his own fallibilities, for his own Midwestern complacency, his propensity for hectoring and militant joylessness," for, in short, "how completely he is a Jonathan Franzen character"[53]—Taffy Brodesser-Akner issues a sharp, smarting correction. A memorable paragraph from her 2018 *Times* profile, "Jonathan Franzen Is Fine with All of It," skewers this aspect of his authorial persona:

> What had he done that was so wrong? Here he was, in his essays and interviews, making informed, nuanced arguments about the way we live now—about anything from Twitter (which he is against) to the way political correctness has been weaponized to shut down discourse (which he is against), to obligatory self-promotion (which he is against) to the incessant ending of a phone call by saying "I love you" (which he is against, but because "I love you" is for private)—and though critics loved him and he had a devoted readership, others were using the very mechanisms and platforms that he warned against (like the internet in general and social media in specific) to ridicule him. Hate-pieces, mean hashtags, reductive eye-rolling at his various stances, a nit-picking of every quote. Accusations that he is willing to pontificate but not to listen. Accusations that he's too fragile to face his accusers! Him! Too fragile![54]

Rhetorically, the paragraph unfolds as takedown-by-defense, stretches of its prose swappable with Grossman's *Time*-cover encomia. Its parentheticals, by listing a series of ever-benigner cultural features "which he is against," capture the recursiveness of Franzen's own positions, the cyclical upsets of his career as an author who "(to some controversy) is the symbol (to some controversy) of the White Male Great American Literary Novelist for the 21st Century (to much controversy)."[55] By tracking his thoughts closely and holding them lightly, Brodesser-Akner asserts the fiction writer's prerogative to move into, while retaining a distanced relationship toward, her subject's perspective. By the passage's end, she invites us to hear the Great American Novelist—now hectoring, now hurt—in an ironized free indirect speech that, in repro-ducing his signature aggro-wounded tonal blend ("Him! Too fragile!"), sends it up.

While allowing himself "once" to have been "a very angry person," "still" to "get frustrated by simple-minded thinking," prone to "go off on a tear when I'm in the presence of something that seems stupid, things that haven't been thought through," the profile's Franzen maintains that, "in my day-to-day life, I just am not angry." A paragraph later, he lets out "a guttural noise" at a fellow driver's unsignaled turn, sniffing that "people are just so inconsiderate."[56] Whether Franzen pilots his hybrid Camry with Cool Ranch composure or white-knuckled ire is immate-rial; his brand is anger, and it's among the strongest in the biz.

For the on-fence Franzen enthusiast, *Succession* has it all: songbirds chomped off five-star flatware; a single, aghast Midwesterner, whom habit and temperament have typed "Mr. Good," tempted to try "Mr. Bad" for a spell (*Freedom*, 481); the descriptor "nice" batted aside as "a horrible thing to say about anyone."[57] Of the would-be successors, it's Connor Roy to whom Brodesser-Akner's portrait of Franzen most closely corresponds. As his siblings—toppled scion Kendall, subzero Shiv, chaos agent Roman—crowd and connive to move phototropically closer to scant rays of parental favor, Connor claims a bystander's neu-trality to their fray, only to employ militarized figures of speech that countervail his stated attitude of stanceless chill. All but invariably, declarations follow disengagements: "I just wanted to say I'm not get-ting involved, but Shiv's right"; "I don't take sides—but I'm on your side." "I don't care, I just observe. I'm a UN white helmet"—but "some-times a peacekeeper has to go shoot a maniac on the perimeter, okay?"[58]

That the "process guy" who works "with no attachment to the out-come," devoted solely to "the thing you can control, which is your own writing," who has softened toward TV, goes misty-eyed over *The Kill-ing*'s finale, attributes his apoplectic public persona to "a younger me in full prosecutorial mode," remains the pugilist railing against "an age when the novel is in retreat and people are looking not to have to read a book," still self-identifies as "a partisan of the novel," wills his works to "defeat all attempts to put them on the screen," shares his agent's puzzlement as to "when exactly they all turned on him";[59] that the writer who, despite being "Fine with All of It," titularly so, also isn't—gets riled, retrenches; to the Franzen fanatic, this isn't surprising, any more than an almost-famously childless writer choosing to compose multigenerational family sagas about climate activists who reproduce at "demographically deplorable" young ages (*Freedom*, 492), then lose sleep tallying population-growth stats.

Franzen possesses writerly equipment—even recognizes an authorial obligation—to inquire, in Reddit-board parlance, "Am I the Asshole?" Literature, in his view, "invites you to ask whether you might be somewhat wrong, maybe even entirely wrong, and to imagine why someone else might hate you."[60] Itself an introduction to the Franzen-curated 2016 volume of *Best American Essays*, "The Essay in Dark Times" unfolds as a process story: part career retrospective of his multidecade editorial collaboration with the *New Yorker*'s Henry Finder, part Jacob-wrestling self-portrait of an author trying, despite his own vitriolic streak, to assay.

Assessing a hotter initial take on the material that would become "Carbon Capture" (2015), Finder "gently suggested I lose the tone of prophetic scorn" and embrace a "more ambivalent, less polemical" mode, issuing successive sets of edits that "nudged me toward framing the essay not as a denunciation but as a question." Finished, the essay's mirror nevertheless "reflected an angry bird-loving misfit who thinks he's smarter than the crowd," a "character" who "may be me, but it's not the whole me." Even as he rues the imagined "better essay," in which "I would have found my way to more sympathy for the people I was angry at," the actual Franzen protests that criticism characterized "Carbon Capture" as a "crime against orthodoxy," frames disparaging responses to the piece as "a missile attack from the liberal silo" that sought to "negate me as a person."[61]

For readers inclined to stare down the author's doom-mongering propensity and conclude "that this is just such bullshit," the way "it's always the death of this and the death of that," *The Corrections* supplies a surrogate in Melissa, a student in Consuming Narratives, Chip Lambert's lit-theory course (*Corrections*, 44). As "things are getting better and better for women and people of color, and gay men and lesbians, more and more integrated and open," she fumes, "all you can think about is some lame, stupid problem with signifiers and signifieds" (44). "Cut to the quick" by Melissa's assessment, Chip laments that "criticizing a sick culture, even if the criticism accomplished nothing, had always felt like useful work. But if the supposed sickness wasn't a sickness at all," "if it was only straight white males like Chip who had a problem with this order—then there was no longer even the most abstract utility to his criticism" (45).

Chip takes Melissa's note, but not for a long time. His "great revelation," when it comes, concerns "The Academy Purple," an exercise in authorial score-settling featuring as protagonist the sexually spurned, conspired-against ex-scholar who proxies for Chip's most self-serving view of his firing from D— college for his treatment of Melissa herself. Where he'd once "imagined he could remove certain hackneyed plot elements—the conspiracy, the car crash, the evil lesbians—and still tell a good story" (90), he now recognizes the failure of his oft-revised script, the reason "why nobody, including himself, had ever liked his screenplay": he'd "written a thriller where he should have written farce" (534).

The generic failure he identifies rests on another, of tone; the irony necessary to achieve escape velocity from his own perceptions' confines cannot be achieved without an attendant shift in perspective, an unblending of authorial point of view from that of focal character. Newly able to stand aside from the tragic self-conception of his textual surrogate, Bill Quaintence, "he bore down with a mental red pencil" on his mental facsimile of the screenplay's opening monologue, "made a little trim here, added emphasis or hyperbole there," until "the scenes became what they'd wanted to be all along: ridiculous," their protagonist refashioned as "a comic fool" (534).

Like "Carbon Capture," "My Bird Problem" casts Franzen as "an angry bird-loving misfit who thinks he's smarter than the crowd," but one who has heeded the feedback to "make it *ridiculous*" (*Corrections*, 534). Indeed, in both content and form, the persuasive limitations of bombast obsess "My Bird Problem." "Expecting to be amused by the speech's rhetorical badness—to roll my eyes at Gore's intoning of 'fate' and 'mankind,' his flaunting of his wonk credentials, his scolding of American consumers," Franzen instead finds himself disarmed at Gore's seeming "to have rediscovered a sense of humor," delivering a speech as "fun to listen to" as it was "unbelievably depressing."[62]

The essay's speaker likewise avails himself of—and impales himself upon—the novelist's ironizing toolkit. Comically outsize metaphors monitor the health of "our marital planet," compare Franzen and his ex-wife to "those habit-bound peoples in Jared Diamond's *Collapse* who respond to an ecosystem's degradation by redoubling their demands on it," while passages of free indirect speech read like rehearsals for the self-deprecation of Patty's autobiographer. "How different my marriage might have been," Franzen laments, "if I'd been able to go birding! How much more tolerable our year in Spain might have been made by European waterfowl!" Elsewhere in *The Discomfort Zone*, Franzen wonders "why 'cartoonish' remains such a pejorative. It took me half my life to achieve seeing my parents as cartoons. And to become more perfectly a cartoon myself: what a victory that would be."[63]

If we were to accept Ship's proposition that "abandoning metaphor is contraindicated," to heed Sontag's urging to "give . . . back to the warmakers" those military metaphors, what other stories might figurative language tell about fiction's future? Herself the subject, a few years earlier, of James Wood's state-of-fiction alarum against "hysterical realism,"[64] Zadie Smith, in "Two Paths for the Novel" (2008), offers one alternative. Assessing an "ailing literary culture" with the essayist's favored diagnostic tool, the metaphor, she at times employs rhetorical escalation and zero-summing common to death-of-the-novel discourse: "literary realism," if it "survived the assault of Joyce," still "retains the wound"; Joseph O'Neill's *Netherland* appears "so precisely the image of what we have been taught to value in fiction that it throws that image into a kind of existential crisis, as the photograph gifts a nervous breakdown to the painted portrait."[65]

Yet "Two Paths for the Novel" audibly considers and ultimately rejects the most extreme of these metaphors. "In its brutal excision of psychology," Smith writes, "it is easy to feel that [Tom McCarthy's 2005 novel] *Remainder* comes to literature as an assassin, to kill the novel stone dead. I think it means rather to shake the novel out of its present complacency. It clears away a little of the dead wood, offering a glimpse of an alternate road down which the novel might, with difficulty, travel forward." What might have been construed by another writer as attempted murder, Smith describes as an act of pruning or trail maintenance, further evidence that "though manifestoes feed on rupture, artworks themselves bear the trace of their own continuity."[66]

Another example, by the novelist Jon McGregor, literally grounds the figure. Asked by an interviewer to predict what his "field will look like twenty-five years from now," McGregor slyly replies that "the fruit orchard will be gnarled and mature," "the walnut and hazelnut trees will just be beginning to soar," "the willow plantation in the boggy corner will be cropping regularly," "the wildflowers will be flowering earlier every year." His future casts the novelist not as a defeated soldier or a defiant revolutionary but as the devoted tender of a particular, earthbound plot, the craftsperson who derives a "locally-famous line of chutney" from its fruits and "still won't quite have got the hang of basket-weaving," the observer who jots a "long-planned memoir on the art of the smallholding."[67]

In adrienne maree brown's *Emergent Strategy*—both a praxis-oriented toolkit inspired by and a philosophical inquiry into the Earthseed principles of Octavia Butler's Parable novels—the author notes that "the natural world actually supports any worldview—competitive, powerless, isolationist, violent." "Humans so far," she observes, "have generally deified and aligned with the 'king' of the jungle or forest—lions, tigers, bears," which, "for all their isolated ferocity and alpha power, are going extinct." In place of these reflexive assumptions, brown advocates for conscious, reflective realignment with and revaluing of "the adaptation of small, collaborative species," among them "roaches and ants and deer and fungi and bacteria and viruses and bamboo and eucalyptus and squirrels and vultures and mice and mosquitoes and dandelions and so many other more collaborative life forms" that, as these hierarchy-topping predators perish, "continue to proliferate, survive, grow."[68]

Given the cultural purchase of his doomsday prophesies for fiction, it's easy to forget the dissatisfaction Franzen has expressed with common metaphors for fiction writing, especially those that mythologize the novelist as a solitary, detached genius. "My small hope for literary criticism," he wrote in 2002, "would be to hear less about orchestras and subversion and more about the erotic and culinary arts." He enjoins fellow critics to "think of the novel as lover"—one concerned with readerly pleasure, aware that "before a book can change you, you have to love it"—or to picture "the novelist as a cook who prepares, as a gift to the reader, this many-course meal."[69] These acts of generosity and care portray the relationship between author and reader in starkly different terms than the novel's with other storytelling forms, occupy other imaginative worlds altogether than the hellscapes where novel writing faces annihilation.

In "a culture that privileges novelty and growth over the cyclical and the regenerative," the former "routinely valorized, not to mention masculinized," the latter often "unrecognized, because it has no part in 'progress,'" Jenny Odell sees maintenance arts as one potential "antidote to the rhetoric of growth."[70] In some modes, at some moments, Franzen sounds this note: the essayist who submits for fiction the working definition of "the transmutation of experiential dross into linguistic gold," alchemically "taking up whatever the world had abandoned by the road and making something beautiful out of it." Viewed this way, his "triumphant return home with scavenged loot—snow shovels, the business end of a broken rake, floor lamps, still-viable poinsettias, aluminum cookware—was as much a part of writing fiction as the typing up of final drafts," "an old phone . . . as much a character in a narrative as an appliance in a home."[71]

"Use and abandonment," he writes, in a sentence from the essay "Scavenging" that could have been pulled from *How to Do Nothing*, "are the aquifer through which consumer objects percolate, shedding the taint of mass production and emerging as historied individuals." In obsolescence, "the leading product of our national infatuation with technology," the author has come to see "not a darkness but a beauty: not perdition but salvation." For this writer, his determination to "just keep doing the same old kind of book" expresses not—or not only—aesthetic conservatism but care for, conservation of, what is, whether a beloved literary form or a discarded but refurbishable article of furniture. "My rotary was losing its ability to cope with the modern world," as he puts it, poignantly, "but I continued to cover for it and to keep it on display downstairs, because I loved it and was afraid of change."[72]

7

COMING DOWN ON FRANZEN (2)

At what point, he wanted to know, could a manuscript still become something entirely different?

Was there time to write another *libellus* altogether—to double, or to halve its length, or keep the number of words unchanged but alter, Argo-like, each one?

There were, after all, so many books he hadn't written: the deep dive on Jonathan Franzen and climate change, the Franzen-Wallace friend-ship tour, the analysis he could have added had he just read *Robinson Crusoe* once more, *Middlemarch* again, *V.* ever, had he only made a last pass through *Twenty-Seventh City*, *Crossroads*, even, heaven forfend, those *Kraus Project* footnotes.

If he labored only a little longer—an afternoon, a lunar month, a year and a day—could he not produce one of those others?

There was the Franzen book with the section about omniscience in *The Overstory*, the one where he put those stray grafs on *The Princess of Cleves* back in, the version with an opinion on whether *MISTAKES WERE MADE* constituted autofiction, the one whose pages pondered whether Jonathan Franzen and Sally Rooney were not, perhaps, so different underneath.

Had he simply not spent enough time reading *Freedom*, was that the issue?

When he weighed the solidity of what he had actually authored—a stack of double-sided sheets the thickness of deck of cards, which a person could take in hand, could riffle, tamp, tear—against those other, entirely speculative works, did he not feel some measure of content-ment, even relief, at having written this one precisely, this one only? Peace, did it descend, to bless things as they were?

He did not; it never did.

Instead, they kept after him, the spectral books: the ones that were gayer, much self-helpier, way more sci-fi. There was the even more novel-istic draft and the *Franzen sans Franzen* edit that refrained, in *Garfield Minus Garfield* fashion, from quoting—even from *referring to*—Franzen at all.

For no reason he could comprehend, the proliferation of these possible works had little effect, far less than he would have expected, on the actual book—the one that ran on string cheese, Trader Joe's dark roast by the carafe, and repeat renditions of twangy Waxahatchee tracks; the manuscript dispersed among scarcely numerable Word docs or gathered into a single, scribbled-over draft—which, whatever his schemes, his fantasies, his pacts with improbability, kept on existing, stayed pretty much itself.

It was astonishing, really, how even the most expansive of his plans for its improvement appeared not to budge the scuffed manila envelope of printed pages one smidge across the Naugahyde top of the ottoman onto which he'd deposited it.

At the same time, the perfect, correct, right book—the one toward which no soul would bear any ill will, that gave no offense, produced no bad effects, displeased nobody; the irrefutable one that would be greeted in every quarter with a nod of benediction—had a strange, stubborn way of never coming into being. If anything, it drew, with time's passage, almost asymptotically farther away.

Was living what you did once you set aside Jonathan Franzen, or were you only through with Jonathan Franzen when you were through with life, or was being alive this disagreeable push-pull between that pair of convictions about Jonathan Franzen? Would it always feel like this? Did he like this guy, or no?

"You really like to wring a topic," remarked a friend, accurately.

Was there any point in doing this? Would it be better never to have begun, to have given up sooner, to have continued until actual became ideal, however long that took?

After all, what sort of book about Franzen was possible when you had set so many tools aside: were unwilling to explain, declined to advance any thesis, refused to render judgments, would not dream of saying what anyone should or shouldn't think of, or do about, Jonathan Franzen? When you only reiterated ceaselessly your own reluctance to come down?

If you wanted to learn something about what was called "your stuff," you could train at worse gymnasia than the one-sidedness of your relationship with—*to*—an American novelist in his sixties who had won the James Tait Black Memorial Prize.

Those aware of his attempts to plait his dissonant Franzen feelings into a monograph would sometimes inquire what he thought Franzen would think about the book—would JF read it, how would Franz react?

Jonathan Franzen, he felt certain, would not lift one grey brow. No more could he have involved the author of *The Corrections* in his interior quarrel than riled K2.

He listened to an algorithmically astute playlist called "Confidence Boost," clearly curated for the freshly broken-up, head-bopped along with its danceable anthems to self-sufficiency, and thought about Jonathan Franzen.

His best friend had recently taught him the expression "to live rent free in one's mind," a phrase that described precisely the terms under which he had offered Franzen residence in his own mental abode—which idiom, he noted with interest, peppered the playlist's tracks. Lizzo had better things to do, he could only assume, than fixate on Franzen. To have cast *Purity* aside as casually as Icona Pop and Charli XCX dismissed the addressee of "I Love It"—on the irrefutable grounds that "you're from the seventies / but I'm a nineties bitch"—bliss, this would have been.

When Taylor voiced that it was "so nice, / so peaceful and quiet," having "forgot that you existed," sang-spoke of an emotion that "isn't love, it isn't hate, it's just indifference," his ears pricked. The lyrics didn't refer specifically to Jonathan Franzen so much as they sounded Franzen-competent, attested to a high degree of Franzen-transferrable skill. They suggested someone who, however rivalrous, feud prone, *Reputation* obsessed, had, in this instance at least, shaken it off so thoroughly as to have rippled once more into calm. And, honestly, that did sound nice.

As for Franzen: on Taylor, where did he come down? Fielding readers' queries at a reading, he'd stated that "I'm not a student of Taylor Swift" and, beyond a vague appreciation for her advocacy of "artists getting properly paid for their work," held "no strong feelings" about her.[1] What strange equanimity was this? Having spent angst-ridden years *in full prosecutorial mode*, JF claimed subsequently to have learned to *devote yourself to the thing you can control, which is your own writing* (Brodesser-Akner).[2]

He conjured an image of himself, correspondingly tranquil, composed, cucurbit-cool. Whatever happened—however stridently the *Crossroads* flap copy claimed that Franzen had been "universally recognized as the leading novelist of his generation," whatever errantry JF next inked into the *New Yorker*'s columns, whoever texted for confirmation of, or comment on, the latest avian debacle—these antics wouldn't faze or flummox him. His shoulders, should they tense, would ease again: a shrug.

"Jonathan Franzen's doing his thing," he'd answer, in tones purloined from Glenn Close's silken Marquise de Merteuil, "and I'm doing mine." With the soft click of a compact, the subject would shut.

However nice this might have been, it didn't come to pass. No *How I Learned to Stop Worrying and Love Jonathan Franzen* arrived to subtitle his anxious Franzephile's *Confessions*. Instead, he stayed himself: a fretful roil whom epidermis scarcely encased.

And yet: you couldn't say, precisely, that nothing had shifted. During that season Maine passed through in lieu of spring, scarcely warmer than it had been, almost as warm as it was getting, stick quickened somehow into stem, whatever budded did so under drift. Having dedicated considerable resources to developing what scanned as somebody, an insensate avatar, it was a disaster—and, however unsought, a thrill—to be rendered *so* visible, *so* visible (*Purity*, 4).

To have someone name a definite point around which the rest of oneself could constellate—"Jonathan Franzen, obsession with"—to realize that, however revulsive, however perplexing, there was something there to see: it felt vernal on the forearms, an electrical prickle where there'd seemed no nerves at all.

This sensation arose, unmistakably, from the operation "shuck," as pried an oyster or exposed an ear of maize: shell lips pulled apart, sheaths of silk and husk stripped away. Inside, to discover—what? He'd ruther kernels in their bright, taut, dental array, but suspected contents closer to nearly liquid viscera, a slick purse of muscle, part stomach, part heart, afloat in its salt pool.

It was a strange thing to feel, but he definitely felt it, sensed himself becoming *a different person, one he could see . . . so clearly, it was like standing outside himself.* Though *this wasn't the person he'd thought he was, or would have chosen to be if he'd been free to choose,* a long-term inhabitant of nowhere might yet find *something comforting and liberating about being an actual definite someone, rather than a collection of contradictory potential someones* (*Freedom,* 432).

He liked Franzen, *in spite of everything; he couldn't help it* (*Freedom,* 244). Even when he thought the man had *been a total asshole, hating* him didn't *seem to be an option* (*Freedom,* 439).

He'd always been a dreamy bastard, tugged by fantasies' strong force, atilt at alter egos and otherwheres. Nothing compelled him less than what was called *the real world,* a phrase he rarely delivered without scare quotes' crooked digits, a skeptical vocal catch. "You are not in reality about this," his mom often said, and he'd never wanted to hear it, not once, even the times she'd been right. Any image in the mind, even a nightmare, even an illusion, he preferred.

Lately, though, he'd started to wonder what it would mean to become a realist, too—someone who vests interest in actuality, who tends the garden of what is.

At the same time, he'd gotten curious about this ravenous creature that pinned him to earth. *Am I alive?,* he'd begun to wonder; *Do I possess a body?* (*Freedom,* 161).

Though this self of his seemed, in temporal terms, almost wholly worry; however like a needle traveling over grooved rumination he felt; no matter the percentage of his inner life occupied by fruitless yet frenzied attempts at such impossibilities as time travel, telepathy, prognostication; he was, at least by mass, more meat than thought.

His thoughts weighed less than an aspirin tablet, while his body was an animal, warm for now, thirteen stone of hair, skin, viscera, muscle, fluid, bone.

The hour you gnawed your own haunch passed, as any other did. While mind whirred, flesh caught: gut growled, bladder whined. Scum scrimmed the dishes, plants withered for want of a soak, pets' fond nudges touched a numb limb.

Copies of *Crossroads* blocked the door, a pulp drift; piled pavers of *Purity* and *Freedom* and *Corrections* bricked over a whole room.

Where he'd once *imagined that he could remove certain hackneyed plot elements—the conspiracy, the car crash, the evil lesbians—and still tell a good story* (*Corrections*, 90), nothing now seemed less likely.

And yet: was there not a tang of irony, one he became better able to detect, even to savor, in being the sort of person who labored in agony over the corrections to his Franzen manuscript without realizing that *he'd written*—well, whatever one called this—*where he should have written farce* (*Corrections*, 534)?

Was it possible that, if he only *made a little trim here, added emphasis or hyperbole there*, these *scenes* could become *what they'd wanted to be all along: ridiculous*, his autofictional avatar *a comic fool* (*Corrections*, 534)?

On reflection, it was astonishing to think he'd ever viewed them any other way.

What else could you have made of a person who stationed himself at your elbow, fixed on your face a look of fascination like Stendhal's at a fresco, and conversed principally in phrases such as "Oh really?" and

"Tell me more about that," in the manner of an unqualified therapist you had not, in fact, requested to see?

Mightn't it even have been quite disconcerting, to speak into the searching gaze of someone who ricocheted so suddenly from Helga Pataki's hard-shelled seethe to the spooked-and-spooky skittishness of Laney Boggs?

Wasn't the D-deficient way he sunned under their attention, however casual, craned toward their approval, however distant, even *a little weird and intense* in retrospect (*Freedom*, 68)?

Consonant with his *experience of crushes—the feeling of inferiority, the hope of being found worthy nonetheless* (*Purity*, 454)—did these tableaux not reveal *a kind of parasite, trying to feel cooler and better about himself by means of his unique connection to* them (*Freedom*, 137)?

He remembered his apartment, rarely farther than blocks away: cherry seltzer by the liter, the better part of a *Broad City* season yet unwatched, a bath enhanced by a daub of that face mask he liked, whose scent and texture were a mint field's after a downpour. He saw how, rather than returning there, he'd assumed the posture of a living interrogative: torqued his neck to an angle of maximum attentiveness, clenched till it cricked.

He noticed that, to disguise his true feelings for Jonathan Franzen, he'd adopted an unusual technique: spoke of little else, allowed this novelist to assume the weather's proximity to small talk, treated his books as the black hole around which, with Gargantua's gravitation, matter settled, minutes stretched.

When, at any mention of the author of *Freedom*, he cast his eyes skyward, let out a little huff of annoyance, who could say what he thought?

Reviewing mental footage of those Franzen-centric conversational forays, he regarded the interlocutors: briskly interrupting after a few sentences, staring at some middle-distant patch that hovered apparition-like over and beside his head, eventually stepping away "for a minute."

To have been the person who'd once regarded these fully scrutable actions as symptomatic, not of the interlocutors' *low to moderate interest* (*Freedom*, 157) in his blather, but of a politesse so arcane, a fascination so specialized, as to require deciphering—it was piquant, zesty, bitter, briny, hot, and, at last, distinctly sweet.

But then, in those days, he was always tasting things he'd never noticed before. "Is this chicken?" he'd wondered, chewing the ciabatta-sandwiched protein he'd eaten for dozens of prior lunches. It seemed to have altogether too much taste, or too many tastes, to act on tongue and teeth as neon broke over, strobes strafed his eyes.

He forgot where he was. Forgot the continent, forgot the year, forgot the time of day, forgot the circumstances. His brain at the counter *was piscine or amphibian, registering impressions, reacting to the moment. He wasn't far from terror. At the same time, he felt OK* (*Corrections*, 538).

Gradually, his person was becoming less the chartless, unkennable tract between the hitch of a tote bag's strap and Blundstones' pull loops than someplace fairly specifically soft and sturdy, coordinates at which he found he quite wanted to stay.

A few minutes a day, a few hours a week, being where and when he was had begun yielding him a *little taste of eternity*, stretches of feeling as if he'd *taken some powerful drug that wasn't wearing off*, or *fallen into an incredibly vivid dream*, while remaining *fully aware, from second to second to second, that it wasn't a drug or a dream but just life happening to* him, *a life with only a present and no past* (*Freedom*, 130).

Via the gunny-sack sexiness of a sleeveless jumpsuit he'd recently acquired, he publicized his possession of a live pulse and a couple of shoulder blades, and recognized himself. He swam decorously paced laps, stomped circles round cemetery paths, seasonally mossed and rimed, and recognized himself. As he sat for tattoos, felt every inked pinprick, he *recognized* himself *as a living person and was*, at times, quite *breathless with the happiness of living* (*Corrections*, 500).

He'd begun to wonder whether however long you had left was always, if not a lifetime, at least a significant interval, a quantity not to be discounted. He *was*, after all, only thirty-five, *and* he *was going to make some changes in* his *life* (*Corrections*, 566).

ACKNOWLEDGMENTS

For their superb editorial guidance and discerning feedback at every stage, I'm indebted to Jenny Davidson, Nick Dames, and Philip Leventhal, as well as Monique Briones, Rob Fellman, Michael Haskell, and the peer reviewers whose reports shaped—and vastly improved—this project.

Faculty Development funds and an Assistant Professorship Award from Saint Joseph's College, of which I'm deeply appreciative, supported this research.

To my students, whose commitment to the reading and interpretation of literary texts consistently inspires and humbles me, I give sincere thanks.

Finally, I wish to express my profound gratitude for the generous listening, shrewd questions, and insightful commentary I received from my loved ones throughout the years I spent writing this book. Particular mentions are owed to Rachel, a fellow Franzen fanatic; those I'm fortunate to cocreate book clubs with, especially Seth and Dominic; my parents, for their unstinting support; and the friends whose conversations and check-ins over the long haul have seen this protracted, seemingly endless composition process through, especially Genna, Hannah, Dana, Laura, Cathy, Gabriel, Sarah, YeYe, and John.

NOTES

1. COMING DOWN ON FRANZEN

1. Frank Herbert, *Dune* (New York: Penguin, 1990), 150.

2. "AH, BUT UNDERNEATH"

1. *Desperate Housewives*, season 1, episode 1, "Pilot," created by Marc Cherry, aired October 3, 2004, ABC.
2. Gillian Flynn, *Gone Girl* (New York: Crown, 2012), 265.
3. *Big Little Lies*, season 1, episode 1, "Somebody's Dead," created by David E. Kelley, aired February 19, 2017, HBO.
4. B. R. Myers, "Smaller Than Life," *Atlantic*, October 2020, theatlantic.com /magazine/archive/2010/10/smaller-than-life/308212/; Terry Gross and Jonathan Franzen, "Franzen Tackles Suburban Parenting in *Freedom*," *Fresh Air*, NPR, September 30, 2011, https://www.npr.org/2011/09/30/140917050 /franzen-tackles-parenting-in-freedom.
5. Jesús Blanco Hidalga, *Jonathan Franzen and the Romance of Community* (New York: Bloomsbury, 2017), 170.
6. Jocelyn Zorn, the praxis-inclined antagonist of Walter's conservation plot, inspires similar ire, though Walter's perspective filters her portrayal more audibly than any character's does Merrie's. Zorn—a "scarily motivated activist" (294) whose name, like a deity out of Homer, comes epithet-paired (as in "nutcase Jocelyn Zorn" [302], "this idiot Jocelyn Zorn" [324]) or cortege-attended ("Zorn and her zealots" [342], "Zorn and some of her women" [338])—installs roadblocks, both literal and figurative, to Walter's environmentally dubious mountaintop-removal scheme. Described as

"pallid and dull-eyed and somewhat macrocephalic-looking," Zorn is nevertheless "the sort of bitter salad green for which Walter ordinarily had a fondness" (338), suggesting that, had she only made herself more agreeable, she might have been entitled to condescension rather than rage. With fondness like this, one wonders, who needs distaste?

7. Ta-Nehisi Coates, *Between the World and Me* (New York: Spiegel & Grau, 2015), 11.

8. Stephen J. Burn and Jonathan Franzen, "Jonathan Franzen—The Art of Fiction No. 207," *Paris Review* 195, https://www.theparisreview.org/interviews /6045/jonathan-franzen-the-art-of-fiction-no-207-jonathan-franzen.

9. In their essay "Letting Go of Innocence" (2019), Prentis Hemphill uses a transformative justice lens to analyze how notions of guilt and innocence are racialized: https://prentishemphill.com/blog/2019/7/5/letting-go-of -innocence.

10. Kai Cheng Thom summarizes this pervasive cultural myth in the following way: "White women are assumed to be inherently innocent. The ideological 'innocence' I speak of here not only refers to the literal 'not guilty of wrongdoing' but also encompasses a sense of 'purity' or 'virtue' that makes it blasphemous or deeply evil to be accused of harming a white woman. This, of course, is part of a historical legacy of the use of white womanhood as a justification for violence against people of colour—not too long ago, it was common for men of colour, especially Black men, to be lynched or imprisoned for supposedly endangering the virtue of white women, a practice that continues in more covert forms to this day." Kai Cheng Thom, *I Hope We Choose Love: A Trans Girl's Notes from the End of the World* (Vancouver: Arsenal Pulp, 2019), 86.

11. Imara Jones, "Transphobia, White Fear, and Elections," *TransLash*, September 3, 2020. Wright's remarks complement his conversation on WNYC's *The United States of Anxiety* with the historian Kwame Holmes, who describes "the absolute power that parents can wield over their children's innocence, their right to control that becomes the rationale for segregationist patterns of movement in and out of cities." Kai Wright, "Scared in the Suburbs," *United States of Anxiety*, WNYC, August 31, 2020, https://www .wnycstudios.org/podcasts/anxiety/episodes/scared-suburbs.

12. Jonathan Franzen, "How He Came to Be Nowhere," *Granta*, June 20, 1996, https://granta.com/how-he-came-to-be-nowhere/.

13. Franzen, "How He Came to Be Nowhere."

14. Christopher Connery and Jonathan Franzen, "The Liberal Form: An Interview with Jonathan Franzen," *boundary 2* 36, no. 2 (2009): 39–42.

15. Isaac Chotiner and Jonathan Franzen, "Jonathan Franzen on Fame, Fascism, and Why He Won't Write a Book About Race," *Slate*, July 31 2016, http://www.slate.com/articles/interrogation/2016/07/a_conversation_with _novelist_jonathan_franzen.html.

16. Toni Morrison, *Playing in the Dark: Whiteness and the Literary Imagination* (New York: Vintage, 1993), 44–45, 52.

17. Maggie Nelson, *On Freedom: Four Songs of Care and Constraint* (Minneapolis: Graywolf, 2021), 3.

18. Amitav Ghosh, *The Great Derangement* (Chicago: University of Chicago Press, 2017), 121.

19. Morrison, *Playing in the Dark*, 45.

3. AGNOSTIC OMNISCIENCE

1. Natalia Ginzburg, *The Little Virtues* (New York: Arcade, 2013), 97.

2. George Eliot, *Middlemarch* (New York: Penguin, 2003), 9, 10.

3. Eliot, *Middlemarch*, 9.

4. *Interstellar*, dir. Christopher Nolan (2014).

5. "The Future of American Fiction," *Charlie Rose*, May 17, 1996, https:// charlierose.com/videos/15361.

6. Jérémy Potier and Jonathan Franzen, "An Interview with Jonathan Franzen," *Transatlantica* 1 (2017), http://journals.openedition.org/transatlantica /8943.

7. Jonathan Franzen, *The Discomfort Zone* (New York: Picador, 2006), 122.

8. Stephen J. Burn and Jonathan Franzen, "Jonathan Franzen—The Art of Fiction No. 207," *Paris Review* 195, https://www.theparisreview.org /interviews/6045/jonathan-franzen-the-art-of-fiction-no-207-jonathan -franzen.

9. Eliot, *Middlemarch*, 194.

10. Shirley Jackson, *The Haunting of Hill House* (New York: Penguin, 2013), 3.

11. Jonathan Franzen, "How He Came to Be Nowhere," *Granta*, June 20, 1996, https://granta.com/how-he-came-to-be-nowhere/.

12. Franzen, "How He Came to Be Nowhere."

13. Franzen, "How He Came to Be Nowhere."

14. Potier and Franzen, "An Interview."

15. *Titanic*, directed by James Cameron (1997).
16. Jonathan Franzen, *Farther Away* (New York: Farrar, Straus and Giroux, 2012), 138.
17. Burn and Franzen, "Jonathan Franzen—The Art of Fiction No. 207."
18. Vladimir Nabokov, *Speak, Memory* (New York: Vintage International, 1989), 17.
19. Burn and Franzen, "Jonathan Franzen—The Art of Fiction No. 207."
20. Nicholas Lezard, quoted in Liz Maynes-Aminzade, "The Omnicompetent Narrator from George Eliot to Jonathan Franzen," *Studies in the Novel* 46, no. 2 (Summer 2014): 236.
21. Burn and Franzen, "Jonathan Franzen—The Art of Fiction No. 207."
22. Audrey Niffenegger, *The Time Traveler's Wife* (San Francisco: MacAdam/Cage, 2003), 33, 55, 150.
23. Ann Leckie, *Ancillary Justice* (New York: Orbit, 2013), 244, 252, 207; emphasis Leckie's.
24. N. K. Jemisin, *The Fifth Season* (New York: Orbit, 2015), 172, 446.
25. Ottessa Moshfegh, *Eileen* (New York: Penguin, 2015), 138, 2, 165.
26. Susan Choi, *Trust Exercise* (New York: Henry Holt, 2019), 145.
27. Choi, *Trust Exercise*, 210, 211.
28. Moshfegh, *Eileen*, 82, 78, 7, 8.
29. Choi, *Trust Exercise*, 134, 212.
30. Choi, *Trust Exercise*, 181.
31. Terry Gross and Jonathan Franzen, "Franzen Tackles Suburban Parenting in *Freedom*," *Fresh Air*, NPR, September 30, 2011, https://www.npr.org/2011/09/30/140917050/franzen-tackles-parenting-in-freedom.
32. Alexander Chee, *How to Write an Autobiographical Novel* (New York: Mariner, 2018), 33, 23.
33. Kim Stanley Robinson, *Aurora* (New York: Hachette, 2015), 337, 334.
34. Burn and Franzen, "Jonathan Franzen—The Art of Fiction No. 207."

4. "EVERYONE'S A MORALIST"

1. *Erin Brockovich*, dir. Steven Soderbergh (2000).
2. A less sympathetic introduction to Richard, under whose gaze Patty feels herself to have been "rendered completely two-dimensional" (*Freedom*, 67), might borrow Hannah Gadsby's commentary on the lineage of male artists who view women as little more than "flesh vases for their dick flowers." *Nanette*, written and performed by Hannah Gadsby (Netflix, 2018).

3. Jonathan Franzen, *Crossroads* (New York: Farrar, Straus and Giroux, 2021), 144, 138, 188.

4. David Remnick and Jonathan Franzen, "Jonathan Franzen Talks with David Remnick," *The New Yorker* Festival, July 22 2014, https://www.youtube.com/watch?v=JA2Ajqwc_yQ.

5. Susan Sontag, *Against Interpretation and Other Essays* (New York: Picador, 1966), 52.

6. In "Mr. Difficult," a 2002 essay about William Gaddis, Franzen terms these two theories, or schools, of fiction writing "Status," which holds that "the value of any novel, even a mediocre one, exists independent of whether people are able to enjoy it," and "Contract," whose adherents assert that "a novel deserves a reader's attention only as long as the author sustains the reader's trust." Jonathan Franzen, *How to Be Alone* (New York: Picador, 2002), 239–40.

7. Stephen J. Burn and Jonathan Franzen, "Jonathan Franzen—The Art of Fiction No. 207," *Paris Review* 195, https://www.theparisreview.org/interviews/6045/jonathan-franzen-the-art-of-fiction-no-207-jonathan-franzen.

8. "The Future of American Fiction," *Charlie Rose*, May 17, 1996, https://charlierose.com/videos/15361.

9. Burn and Franzen, "Jonathan Franzen—The Art of Fiction No. 207."

10. Christopher Connery and Jonathan Franzen, "The Liberal Form: An Interview with Jonathan Franzen," *boundary 2* 36, no. 2 (2009): 39.

11. Jérémy Potier and Jonathan Franzen, "An Interview with Jonathan Franzen," *Transatlantica* 1 (2017), http://journals.openedition.org/transatlantica/8943.

12. Jonathan Franzen, *Purity* (New York: Farrar, Straus and Giroux, 2015), 16, 92.

13. Franzen, *Crossroads*, 22, 351, 136, 393, 268, 101.

14. *The Good Place*, season 1, episode 9, ". . . Someone Like Me As a Member," created by Michael Schur, aired November 3, 2016, NBC.

15. *The Good Place*, season 1, episode 1, "Everything Is Fine," created by Michael Schur, aired September 19, 2016, NBC.

16. Kim Stanley Robinson, *Aurora* (New York: Hachette, 2015), 27, 47, 34, 52, 131, 52, 133.

17. Robinson, *Aurora*, 52, 134.

18. "Author Jonathan Franzen Discusses His Collection of Essays, *How to Be Alone*," *Charlie Rose*, October 30, 2002, https://charlierose.com/videos/666.

19. Burn and Franzen, "Jonathan Franzen—The Art of Fiction No. 207."

5. EXILED IN GUYVILLE

1. Ira Glass, "Simulated Worlds," *This American Life*, October 11, 1996, https://www.thisamericanlife.org/38/simulated-worlds.
2. Stephen J. Burn and Jonathan Franzen, "Jonathan Franzen—the Art of Fiction No. 207," *Paris Review* 195, https://www.theparisreview.org/interviews/6045/jonathan-franzen-the-art-of-fiction-no-207-jonathan-franzen.
3. Gérard Genette, *Narrative Discourse: An Essay in Method*, trans. Jane E. Lewin (Ithaca, NY: Cornell University Press, 1983), 189.
4. Jonathan Franzen, *Strong Motion* (New York: Picador, 1992), 359–60.
5. Leo Tolstoy, *War and Peace*, trans. Richard Pevear and Larissa Volokhonsky (New York: Vintage, 2008), 106.
6. Philip K. Dick, *Do Androids Dream of Electric Sheep?* (New York: Del Rey, 1968), 22.
7. Franzen, *Strong Motion*, 102.
8. Jonathan Franzen, *The Discomfort Zone* (New York: Picador, 2006), 23–25.
9. Franzen, *The Discomfort Zone*, 24, 25.
10. Jonathan Franzen, *Purity* (New York: Farrar, Straus and Giroux, 2015), 85, 5.
11. Franzen, *Strong Motion*, 367.
12. Jonathan Franzen, *How to Be Alone* (New York: Picador, 2002), 70.
13. Jonathan Franzen, "How He Came to Be Nowhere," *Granta*, June 20, 1996, https://granta.com/how-he-came-to-be-nowhere/.
14. Franzen, *The Discomfort Zone*, 164.
15. Franzen, *The Discomfort Zone*, 179, 194, 183, 194.
16. Jonathan Franzen, *Farther Away* (New York: Farrar, Straus and Giroux, 2012), 122, 123, 130.
17. George Eliot, *Middlemarch* (New York: Penguin, 2003), 838.
18. Franzen, *The Discomfort Zone*, 145.

6. THE MORE HE FOUGHT ABOUT IT, THE ANGRIER HE GOT

1. "The Future of American Fiction," *Charlie Rose*, May 17, 1996, https://charlierose.com/videos/15361.
2. "The Future of American Fiction."
3. Jonathan Franzen, *How to Be Alone* (New York: Picador, 2002), 61, 63.

4. Donald Antrim and Jonathan Franzen, "Jonathan Franzen by Donald Antrim," *BOMB*, October 1, 2001, https://bombmagazine.org/articles/jonathan -franzen/.

5. Franzen, *How to Be Alone*, 61.

6. Barack Obama and Marilynne Robinson, "President Obama & Marilynne Robinson: A Conversation—II," *New York Review of Books*, November 19, 2015, http://www.nybooks.com/articles/2015/11/19/president-obama -marilynne-robinson-conversation-2/.

7. Lucy Kellaway and Jonathan Franzen, "Lunch with the FT: Jonathan Franzen," *Financial Times*, October 9, 2015, https://www.ft.com/content /6a563a5a-6cde-11e5-8171-ba1968cf791a.

8. Jonathan Franzen, *The Kraus Project* (New York: Farrar, Straus and Giroux, 2013), 110, 112.

9. Franzen, *The Kraus Project*, 110, 111.

10. George Eliot, *Middlemarch* (New York: Penguin, 2003), 85.

11. Franzen, *How to Be Alone*, 164, 196, 80.

12. Franzen, *How to Be Alone*, 67, 165, 88, 172.

13. J. R. R. Tolkien, *The Fellowship of the Ring* (London: HarperCollins, 2008), 419.

14. Franzen, *How to Be Alone*, 62.

15. Franzen, *How to Be Alone*, 196, 199.

16. Ursula Le Guin puts it this way: "War as a moral metaphor is limited, limiting, and dangerous. By reducing the choices of action to 'a war against' whatever-it-is, you divide the world into Me or Us (good) and Them or It (bad) and reduce the ethical complexity and moral richness of our life to Yes/No, On/Off. This is puerile, misleading, and degrading. In stories, it evades any solution but violence and offers the reader mere infantile reassurance. All too often the heroes of such fantasies behave exactly as the villains do, acting with mindless violence, but the hero is on the 'right' side and therefore will win. Right makes might." Ursula Le Guin, "Afterword," in *A Wizard of Earthsea* (New York: Harcourt, 2012), 223.

17. Jonathan Franzen, *The End of the End of the Earth* (New York: Farrar, Straus and Giroux, 2018), 102, 18.

18. Franzen, *How to Be Alone*, 55, 87, 89, 90.

19. Citations come from both the essay's original version, "Perchance to Dream," published in 1996 in *Harper's*, and its updated form, "Why Bother?," as reprinted in *How to Be Alone*. Quotes from the *Harper's* original are followed by an H.

20. The essay's republication as "Why Bother?" (2002) makes the metaphor's autobiographical content and perspectival frame more clear: where the original *Harper's* text had asserted that "the institution of writing and reading serious novels *is like* a grand old Middle American city" (H, emphasis Gibson's), the version released in *How to Be Alone* observes that "the literary America in which I found myself after I published *The Twenty-Seventh City* bore a strange resemblance to the St. Louis I'd grown up in" (*How to Be Alone*, 62).

21. Franzen, *The End of the End of the Earth*, 25, 30.

22. Franzen, *How to Be Alone*, 95, 96, 90, 200.

23. Paul Fussell, *The Great War and Modern Memory* (New York: Oxford University Press, 2013), 24, 23, 204–5.

24. Susan Sontag, "AIDS and Its Metaphors," in *Illness as Metaphor and AIDS and Its Metaphors* (New York: Penguin, 2009), 174, 175, 173.

25. Sontag, "AIDS and Its Metaphors," 179–80.

26. Franzen, *How to Be Alone*, 59.

27. Franzen, *How to Be Alone*, 164–65.

28. Franzen, *How to Be Alone*, 195, 199.

29. Ali Smith, *Winter* (New York: Pantheon, 2018), 3–4.

30. Oscar Wilde, *The Importance of Being Ernest and Other Plays* (New York: Oxford World's Classics, 2008).

31. Franzen, *Farther Away* (New York: Farrar, Straus and Giroux, 2012), 30, 34, 33.

32. Franzen, *Farther Away*, 33–35.

33. Franzen, *The End of the End of the Earth*, 38, 39, 22.

34. Sontag, "AIDS and Its Metaphors," 178–9.

35. Amitav Ghosh, *The Great Derangement* (Chicago: University of Chicago Press, 2017), 8, 27, 11, 35, 17, 71.

36. Stephen J. Burn and Jonathan Franzen, "Jonathan Franzen—The Art of Fiction No. 207," *Paris Review* 195, https://www.theparisreview.org/interviews/6045/jonathan-franzen-the-art-of-fiction-no-207-jonathan-franzen.

37. Franzen, *Purity* (New York: Farrar, Straus and Giroux, 2015), 196, 203, 197.

38. Franzen, *Purity*, 199, 206, 202, 201.

39. Franzen, *Purity*, 428, 198.

40. Lev Grossman, "Jonathan Franzen: Great American Novelist," *Time*, August 12, 2010, http://content.time.com/magazine/article/0,9171,2010185,00.html.

41. Grossman, "Jonathan Franzen."

42. Grossman, "Jonathan Franzen."

43. Terry Gross and Jonathan Franzen, "Jonathan Franzen on Writing: It's an 'Escape from Everything,'" *Fresh Air*, September 1, 2015, https://www.npr.org/2015/09/01/436442184/jonathan-franzen-on-writing-its-an-escape-from-everything.

44. Grossman, "Jonathan Franzen."

45. Jenny Odell, *How to Do Nothing: Resisting the Attention Economy* (Brooklyn: Melville House, 2019), 137–38.

46. Nicholas Dames, "Franzen Makes Nice," *Public Books*, September 1, 2015, https://www.publicbooks.org/franzen-makes-nice.

47. Chuck Klosterman, "The Jonathan Franzen Award for Jaw-Dropping Literary Genius Goes to . . . Jonathan Franzen," *GQ*, December 3, 2010, https://www.gq.com/story/jonathan-franzen-profile-chuck-klosterman-freedom.

48. "Author Jonathan Franzen Discusses His Collection of Essays, *How to Be Alone*," *Charlie Rose*, October 30, 2002, https://charlierose.com/videos/666.

49. *You've Got Mail*, dir. Nora Ephron (1998).

50. Sigrid Nunez, *The Friend* (New York: Riverhead, 2018), 115.

51. *Russian Doll*, season 1, episode 5, "Superiority Complex," created by Natasha Lyonne, Leslye Headland, and Amy Poehler, aired February 1, 2019, Netflix.

52. *You've Got Mail*.

53. Parul Sehgal, "On *The Twenty-Seventh City* by Jonathan Franzen," *Slate Book Review*, November 8, 2013, https://parulsehgal.com/2013/11/08/the-twenty-seventh-city.

54. Taffy Brodesser-Akner, "Jonathan Franzen Is Fine with All of It," *New York Times Magazine*, June 26, 2018, nytimes.com/2018/06/26/magazine/jonathan-franzen-is-fine-with-all-of-it.html.

55. Brodesser-Akner, "Jonathan Franzen Is Fine with All of It."

56. Brodesser-Akner, "Jonathan Franzen Is Fine with All of It."

57. *Succession*, season 1, episode 6, "Which Side Are You On?," created by Jesse Armstrong, aired July 8, 2018, HBO.

58. *Succession*, season 1, episode 2, "Shit Show at the Fuck Factory," created by Jesse Armstrong, aired June 10, 2018, HBO.

59. Brodesser-Akner, "Jonathan Franzen Is Fine with All of It."

60. Franzen, *The End of the End of the Earth*, 14.

61. Franzen, *The End of the End of the Earth*, 18–19, 22, 19, 19, 20.

62. Franzen, *The Discomfort Zone* (New York: Picador, 2006), 163.

63. Franzen, *The Discomfort Zone*, 169, 165, 182, 50.
64. James Wood, "Human, All Too Inhuman," *New Republic*, July 24, 2000, https://newrepublic.com/article/61361/human-inhuman.
65. Zadie Smith, "Two Paths for the Novel," *New York Review of Books*, November 20, 2008, http://www.nybooks.com/articles/2008/11/20/two-paths-for -the-novel/.
66. Smith, "Two Paths for the Novel."
67. Jon McGregor, "Twenty Questions with Jon McGregor," *Times Literary Supplement*, https://www.the-tls.co.uk/articles/tls-interview-job-mcgregor/.
68. adrienne maree brown, *Emergent Strategy* (Oakland, CA: AK, 2017), 4.
69. Franzen, *How to Be Alone*, 261.
70. Odell, *How to Do Nothing*, 25, 26, 25.
71. Franzen, *How to Be Alone*, 198.
72. Franzen, *How to Be Alone*, 205, 204, 196.

7. COMING DOWN ON FRANZEN (2)

1. Rich Smith, "Jonathan Franzen on Taylor Swift, Binoculars, and *Purity*," *Stranger*, September 10, 2015, https://thestranger.com/blogs/slog/2015/09/10 /22842285/jonathan-franzen-on-taylor-swift-binoculars-and-purity.
2. Taffy Brodesser-Akner, "Jonathan Franzen Is Fine with All of It," *New York Times Magazine*, June 26, 2018, https://nytimes.com/2018/06/26/magazine /jonathan-franzen-is-fine-with-all-of-it.html.

BIBLIOGRAPHY

Antrim, Donald, and Jonathan Franzen. "Jonathan Franzen by Donald Antrim."
    Bomb, October 1, 2001. https://bombmagazine.org/articles/jonathan-franzen/.
"Author Jonathan Franzen Discusses His Collection of Essays, *How to Be Alone*."
    Charlie Rose Show, October 30, 2002. https://charlierose.com/videos/666.
Brodesser-Akner, Taffy. "Jonathan Franzen Is Fine with All of It." *New York Times
    Magazine*, June 26, 2018. https://nytimes.com/2018/06/26/magazine/jonathan
    -franzen-is-fine-with-all-of-it.html.
brown, adrienne maree. *Emergent Strategy*. Oakland, CA: AK, 2017.
Brown, Jeffrey, and Jonathan Franzen. "In 'Purity,' Jonathan Franzen Disman-
    tles the Deception of Idealism." *PBS NewsHour*, September 1, 2015. https://
    www.pbs.org/newshour/show/purity-jonathan-franzen-dismantles-self-decep
    tion-idealism.
Burn, Stephen J., and Jonathan Franzen. "Jonathan Franzen—the Art of Fiction
    No. 207." *Paris Review* 195 (Winter 2010). https://www.theparisreview.org
    /interviews/6045/jonathan-franzen-the-art-of-fiction-no-207-jonathan-franzen.
Chee, Alexander. "The Querent." In *How to Write an Autobiographical Novel*.
    New York: Mariner, 2018.
Choi, Susan. *Trust Exercise*. New York: Henry Holt, 2019.
Chotiner, Isaac, and Jonathan Franzen. "Jonathan Franzen on Fame, Fascism, and
    Why He Won't Write a Book About Race." *Slate*, July 31, 2016. http://www
    .slate.com/articles/interrogation/2016/07/a_conversation_with_novelist_jona
    than_franzen.html.
Coates, Ta-Nehisi. *Between the World and Me*. New York: Spiegel & Grau, 2015.
Connery, Christopher, and Jonathan Franzen. "The Liberal Form: An Inter-
    view with Jonathan Franzen." *boundary 2* 36, no. 2 (2009): 31–54.

Dames, Nicholas. "Franzen Makes Nice." *Public Books*, September 1, 2015. https://www.publicbooks.org/franzen-makes-nice/.

Dick, Philip K. *Do Androids Dream of Electric Sheep?* New York: Del Rey, 1968.

Eliot, George. *Middlemarch.* New York: Penguin, 2003.

Erin Brockovich. Dir. Steven Soderbergh. 2000.

"Everything Is Fine." *The Good Place.* Created by Michael Schur. Season 1, episode 1. NBC, 2016.

Flynn, Gillian. *Gone Girl.* New York: Crown, 2012.

Franzen, Jonathan. *The Corrections.* New York: Farrar, Straus and Giroux, 2001.

——. *Crossroads.* New York: Farrar, Straus and Giroux, 2021.

——. *The Discomfort Zone.* New York: Picador, 2006.

——. *The End of the End of the Earth.* New York: Farrar, Straus and Giroux, 2018.

——. *Farther Away.* New York: Farrar, Straus and Giroux, 2012.

——. *Freedom.* New York: Farrar, Straus and Giroux, 2010.

——. "How He Came to Be Nowhere." *Granta*, June 20, 1996. https://granta.com/how-he-came-to-be-nowhere/.

——. *How to Be Alone.* New York: Picador, 2002.

——. *The Kraus Project.* New York: Farrar, Straus and Giroux, 2013.

——. "Perchance to Dream." *Harper's*, April 1996, 35–54.

——. *Purity.* New York: Farrar, Straus and Giroux, 2015.

——. *Strong Motion.* New York: Picador, 1992.

Fussell, Paul. *The Great War and Modern Memory.* New York: Oxford University Press, 2013.

"The Future of American Fiction." Roundtable discussion featuring Jonathan Franzen, Mark Leyner, and David Foster Wallace. *Charlie Rose Show*, May 17, 1996. https://charlierose.com/videos/15361.

Genette, Gérard. *Narrative Discourse: An Essay in Method.* Trans. Jane E. Lewin. Ithaca, NY: Cornell University Press, 1983.

Ghosh, Amitav. *The Great Derangement.* Chicago: University of Chicago Press, 2017.

Ginzburg, Natalia. "Le piccole virtù." In *The Little Virtues.* New York: Arcade, 2013.

Glass, Ira. "Simulated Worlds." *This American Life*, October 11, 1996. https://www.thisamericanlife.org/38/simulated-worlds.

Gross, Terry. "Franzen Tackles Suburban Parenting in *Freedom*." *Fresh Air*, September 30, 2011. https://www.npr.org/2011/09/30/140917050/franzen-tackles-parenting-in-freedom.

———. "Jonathan Franzen on Writing: It's an 'Escape from Everything.'" *Fresh Air*, September 1, 2015. https://www.npr.org/2015/09/01/436442184/jonathan -franzen-on-writing-its-an-escape-from-everything.

Grossman, Lev. "Jonathan Franzen: Great American Novelist." *Time*, August 12, 2010. http://content.time.com/time/magazine/article/0,9171,2010185,00.html.

Hemphill, Prentis. "Letting Go of Innocence." July 12, 2019. https://prentlsh emphill.com/blog/2019/7/5/letting-go-of-innocence/.

Herbert, Frank. *Dune*. New York: Penguin, 1990.

Hidalga, Jesús Blanco. *Jonathan Franzen and the Romance of Community*. New York: Bloomsbury, 2017.

Interstellar. Dir. Christopher Nolan. 2014.

Jackson, Shirley. *The Haunting of Hill House*. New York: Penguin, 2013.

Jemisin, N. K. *The Fifth Season*. New York: Orbit, 2015.

Jones, Imara. "Transphobia, White Fear, and Elections." *TransLash*, September 3, 2020.

Kellaway, Lucy, and Jonathan Franzen. "Lunch with the FT: Jonathan Franzen." *Financial Times*, October 9, 2015. https://www.ft.com/content/6a563a5a-6cde -11e5-8171-ba1968cf791a.

Klosterman, Chuck. "The Jonathan Franzen Award for Jaw-Dropping Literary Genius Goes to . . . Jonathan Franzen." *GQ*, December 3, 2010. https:// www.gq.com/story/jonathan-franzen-profile-chuck-klosterman-freedom.

Leckie, Ann. *Ancillary Justice*. New York: Orbit, 2013.

LeGuin, Ursula. "Afterword." In *A Wizard of Earthsea*, 218–24. New York: Harcourt, 2012.

Maynes-Aminzade, Liz. "The Omnicompetent Narrator from George Eliot to Jonathan Franzen." *Studies in the Novel* 46, no. 2 (Summer 2014): 236–53.

Morrison, Toni. *Playing in the Dark: Whiteness and the Literary Imagination*. New York: Vintage, 1993.

Moshfegh, Ottessa. *Eileen*. New York: Penguin, 2015.

Myers, B. R. "Smaller Than Life." *Atlantic*, October 2010. theatlantic.com /magazine/archive/2010/10/smaller-than-life/308212/.

Nabokov, Vladimir. *Speak, Memory*. New York: Vintage, 1989.

Nanette. Written and performed by Hannah Gadsby. Netflix, 2018.

Nelson, Maggie. *On Freedom: Four Songs of Care and Constraint*. Minneapolis: Graywolf, 2021.

Niffenegger, Audrey. *The Time Traveler's Wife*. San Francisco: MacAdam/Cage, 2003.

Nunez, Sigrid. *The Friend*. New York: Riverhead, 2018.

Obama, Barack, and Marilynne Robinson. "President Obama & Marilynne Robinson: A Conversation—II." *New York Review of Books*, November 19, 2015. http://www.nybooks.com/articles/2015/11/19/president-obama-marilynne -robinson-conversation-2/.

Odell, Jenny. *How to Do Nothing: Resisting the Attention Economy*. Brooklyn: Melville House, 2019.

"Pilot." *Desperate Housewives*. Created by Marc Cherry. Season 1, episode 1. ABC, 2004.

Potier, Jérémy. "An Interview with Jonathan Franzen." *Transatlantica* 1 (2017). http://journals.openedition.org/transatlantica/8943.

Remnick, David. "Jonathan Franzen Talks with David Remnick." *New Yorker* Festival, July 22, 2014. https://www.youtube.com/watch?v=JA2Ajqwc_yQ.

Robinson, Kim Stanley. *Aurora*. New York: Hachette, 2015.

Sehgal, Parul. "On *The Twenty-Seventh City* by Jonathan Franzen." *Slate Book Review*, November 8, 2013. https://parulsehgal.com/2013/11/08/the-twenty -seventh-city.

"Shit Show at the Fuck Factory." *Succession*. Created by Jesse Armstrong. Season 1, episode 2. HBO, 2018.

Smith, Ali. *Winter*. New York: Pantheon, 2018.

Smith, Rich. "Jonathan Franzen on Taylor Swift, Binoculars, and *Purity*." *Stranger*, September 10, 2015. https://www.thestranger.com/blogs/slog/2015/09/10/2284 2285/jonathan-franzen-on-taylor-swift-binoculars-and-purity.

Smith, Zadie. "Two Paths for the Novel." *New York Review of Books*, November 20, 2008. http://www.nybooks.com/articles/2008/11/20/two-paths-for-the -novel/.

Sontag, Susan. "Camus' Notebooks." In *Against Interpretation and Other Essays*, 52–60. New York: Picador, 1966.

——. *Illness as Metaphor and AIDS and Its Metaphors*. New York: Penguin, 2009.

"Somebody's Dead." *Big Little Lies*. Created by David E. Kelley. Season 1, episode 1. HBO, 2017.

". . . Someone Like Me As a Member." *The Good Place*. Created by Michael Schur. Season 1, episode 9. NBC, 2016.

"Superiority Complex." *Russian Doll*. Created by Natasha Lyonne, Leslye Headland, and Amy Poehler. Season 1, episode 5. Netflix, 2019.

Thom, Kai Cheng. In *I Hope We Choose Love: A Trans Girl's Notes from the End of the World*. Vancouver: Arsenal Pulp, 2019.

Titanic. Dir. James Cameron. 1997.

Tolkien, J. R. R. *The Fellowship of the Ring*. London: HarperCollins, 2008.

Tolstoy, Leo. *War and Peace*. Trans. Richard Pevear and Larissa Volokhonsky. New York: Vintage, 2008

"Twenty Questions with Jon McGregor." *Times Literary Supplement*. https:// www.the-tls.co.uk/articles/tls-interview-jon-mcgregor/.

Wood, James. "Human, All Too Inhuman." *New Republic*, July 24, 2000. https:// newrepublic.com/article/61361/human-inhuman.

"Which Side Are You On?". *Succession*. Created by Jesse Armstrong. Season 1, episode 6. HBO, 2018.

Wilde, Oscar. *The Importance of Being Ernest and Other Plays*. New York: Oxford World's Classics, 2008.

Wright, Kai. "Scared in the Suburbs." *United States of Anxiety*, WNYC, August 31, 2020. https://www.wnycstudios.org/podcasts/anxiety/episodes /scared-suburbs.

You've Got Mail. Dir. Nora Ephron. 1998.

INDEX